DESSERT

DESSERT
A Tale of Happy Endings

JERI QUINZIO

REAKTION BOOKS

To Barbara Ketcham Wheaton and the late Pat Kelly
For their wisdom, generosity and, most of all, friendship.

Published by Reaktion Books Ltd
Unit 32, Waterside
44–48 Wharf Road
London N1 7UX, UK
www.reaktionbooks.co.uk

First published 2018
Copyright © Jeri Quinzio 2018

Printed and bound in China

A catalogue record for this book is available from the British Library

ISBN 978 1 78023 983 5

CONTENTS

A selection of today's splendid pastries.

INTRODUCTION:
THE LOVELY INDULGENCE
OF DESSERT

WHETHER IT'S HOMEMADE strawberry shortcake eaten on a screened porch in summer or a chef's complex medley of delicate pastries served in an elegant restaurant, dessert is the perfect ending to dinner. It is the encore that concludes a wonderful performance and sends us off in a haze of delight. Growing up, dessert was my favourite course. It still is. My dessert might be as simple as a scoop of coffee ice cream or as indulgent as a buttery lemon tart. It doesn't have to be elaborate; it simply has to be. Without it, my dinner would be incomplete and my life would be less sweet.

Some of my best food memories are of desserts. I still recall the intensely fresh peach taste of the ice cream a friend of my parents made for us one summer when I was a child. I remember the brief glow of blue flames on a plum pudding I made one Christmas and how impressive it looked in the darkened room. I can hear the crackling sound my spoon made when it shattered the top of a perfect crème brûlée in Paris and the creaminess beneath its sugar crust. When I think of those desserts, I smile and savour them all over again.

I do understand that consuming too much sugar can result in problems like obesity and diabetes, and that we should not eat it in excess. But much of the sugar we consume is contained in seemingly savoury shop-bought foods. Let us cut down on those and allow ourselves the pleasure and lovely memories desserts offer. I believe a little indulgence is good for the psyche, which is why I wrote this book.

As I was writing, I often asked friends, relatives and acquaintances about their dessert memories and asked, 'What's your favourite dessert?' I thought it would be entertaining to hear what they chose and wondered how similar the choices would be. I was surprised at how seriously they took the question and how thoughtful they became in answering it. It was as if I had asked the classically unanswerable question, 'Which is your favourite child?' Some rather plaintively asked if they could name more than one. Even when I asked them to limit it to one, because favourite means the one most liked rather than one of many liked, they often told me their first choice and then, as if to avoid hurting the feelings of other desserts, they named one or two more.

Although this was certainly not a statistically significant poll, it did include people from several countries and a variety of ethnicities and ages. The answers were not only well considered, they were somewhat surprising. Fewer people than I would have expected chose a chocolate dessert. Where were the chocolate cupcakes, the brownies? Most of the favourites were soft and milky, one of the most ancient dessert categories. Comforting, mother's milk desserts such as crème brûlée, custard pie, tiramisu and various flavours of ice cream led the pack. Many people chose something creamy accompanied by meringue, from lemon meringue pie to pavlova to floating island. Where were the apple pies? Does no one like soufflés? Just two people chose fresh fruit. My favourite dessert is ice cream. My favourite flavour varies according to my mood, the weather, the season and the surroundings.

Most of us have a favourite dessert, even those who seldom indulge. After all, sweet is one of the most basic flavours, and we seem to be hard-wired to like it. However, although everyone does have a taste for sweetness, not every culture enjoys a dessert course at the end of a meal. Nor does each one delight in the sort of dishes most Westerners think of as dessert. Setting aside today's rapid globalization of dining habits, the traditional end to a meal in many countries was and is fruit, whether fresh, dried or cooked in syrup. In medieval times, when fresh fruit was considered unhealthy, Europeans mostly ate fruits dried, like dates or raisins, or cooked in honey or sugar syrup. That tradition lives on in Greece's spoon sweets, which are still a speciality. However, they are generally offered to afternoon guests along with coffee or cold water rather than served as an after-dinner dessert.

The custom of serving sweet dishes as snacks between meals or as celebratory foods, but seldom after a meal, is widespread. The Chinese generally end everyday meals with fresh fruit, and reserve desserts for formal dinners and special occasions. In Japan, sweets are served with tea, but seldom at the close of a meal. In the West, Italians traditionally conclude a meal with fresh fruit and nuts, and enjoy sweet dishes as mid-afternoon treats or holiday specialities. Austrians are likely to go to a pastry shop for indulgences like the cream-filled, chocolate-glazed cakes called *Indianerkrapfen* or *Indianers* in the afternoon, rather than have them after dinner.

Even those who seldom have dessert after everyday dinners do have a favourite holiday dessert. From *capirotada*, Mexico's festive Easter-time bread pudding, to China's autumn festival mooncakes, the holiday dessert is essential to the celebration.

Many desserts we know and love – the ethereal sponge cakes, the lush ice creams, the light and airy profiteroles – are neither as old nor as ubiquitous as they seem. In *Dessert: A Tale of Happy Endings*, I trace the history of dessert, the sweet course served at the end of a meal, and the way it has evolved over time. I begin before dessert was a separate course, when sweets and savouries mixed indiscriminately on the table, and conclude in the present, when homey desserts are enjoying a revival and, at the same time, molecular gastronomists are making desserts an alchemist would envy.

Historically speaking, the serving of a separate dessert course is not an ancient practice. Although the word was used as early as the fourteenth century in France, the course was likely to include savoury dishes as well as sweet ones. The English came to dessert later. The *Oxford English Dictionary*'s first citation of the word is not until 1600, when Sir William Vaughan wrote in *Naturall and Artificiall Directions for Health*, 'such eating, which the French call desert, is unnaturall'. The OED defines dessert as 'a course of fruit, sweetmeats, etc. served after a dinner or supper'.

The term comes from the French word *desservir*, to remove what has been served. In other words, to clear the table. Before the seventeenth century, however, the table was not cleared for the sweet dishes. Foods were not served sequentially: a dozen or so dishes for each course were set out on the table at the same time, in much the way a buffet is today. According to plans illustrated in cookbooks, dishes were symmetrically arranged on the table with similar dishes at either end and on the sides. The centre of the table would feature an impressive dish, which could be anything from a sirloin of beef to a pyramid of sweetmeats. Although each dish was precisely placed, the mix of sweet and savoury was random, according to today's standards. A cherry tart might be placed next to a pigeon pie, a platter of salmon alongside a bowl of custard, buttered turnips beside a selection of marzipans. When one course concluded, a second equally eclectic one would be served. Sweet dishes were scattered throughout cookbooks as well, rather than placed in a separate section.

On special occasions in medieval France, when there was a final serving after the table was cleared, it was usually called an *issue de table*. The spiced wine called *hypocras* would be served as a *digestif*, along with *oublies*, or wafers. Finally *dragées*, or comfits, might be offered. Comfits were sugar-coated seeds or nuts, which were often sprinkled on both savoury and sweet dishes for decoration in addition to being served on their own. They were also eaten as bedtime snacks and as breath-fresheners; in the *Merry Wives of Windsor*, Shakespeare has the lustful Falstaff call for the sky to 'hail kissing-comfits'.

At Renaissance-era feasts, the appearance and entertainment value of foods was at least as prized as their taste. In fact, some of the most impressive dishes were not intended to be eaten. Cooks sculpted towering castles from sugar paste and set them out as centrepieces or focal points on the table. They filled sturdy, standing pies with blackbirds that flew out when the pie was carved, much to the surprise of dinner guests. They moulded realistic-looking fruits and animals from marzipan. When the marzipan sculptures that Leonardo da Vinci created for the court of Ludovico Sforza were gobbled up, Leonardo complained. He had wanted them to be admired, not consumed.

The lofty architectural desserts some pastry chefs create today are part of the same tradition. They are a feast for the eyes but a challenge to eat. Putting a fork to one of these can feel like attacking a work of art with a wrecking ball. As some of their early predecessors did, these pastry chefs value spectacle and display over dining. Flaming desserts, although intended to be eaten and not as spectacular as soaring blackbirds, are also meant to dazzle diners.

Before the eighteenth century, the high cost of sugar and spices made them status symbols, so those who could afford them flaunted them. Many a savoury dish was made with or strewn with sugar. English cooks sweetened their hefty meat pies with sugar and candied fruits. Renaissance-era Italians feasted on tagliatelle tossed with sugar, oranges, cinnamon and almonds and served alongside poultry and meats. Some of these ancient sweet and savoury combinations survive. A festive Iranian rice dish called *shirin polo* is rich with candied orange peel, pistachios, almonds and cinnamon. The ingredients are perfect for a rice pudding, but this is a pilaf made for special occasions and served as part of a meal, not as a dessert. The dessert pudding we call 'blancmange' was once a savoury dish served with the meal rather than after it. It was a mixture of cream and shredded capon, chicken or fish, thickened with grated stag's horn or rice, sweetened and flavoured with almonds. Italians called it *biancomangiare*. In most countries, without the chicken and stag's horn, it became a sweet dessert pudding. In Turkey, where it is called *tavuk göğsü*, it retained the shredded chicken even as it became a dessert.

In the United States, children are usually surprised when they are told that the mincemeat in their Thanksgiving or Christmas pie used to be made with actual minced beef (or venison) along with raisins, apples, spices and brandy. They are even more surprised to learn that in some places mincemeat is still made at home, not purchased at a supermarket, and that meat is still an ingredient.

Eventually, however, most savoury dishes lost their sweet ingredients and most sweet dishes went without their meats. Sweet and savoury went their separate ways, and dessert, both the word and the course, gained widespread acceptance throughout most of Europe. New World ingredients, such as chocolate, entered the marketplace. New equipment such as ovens and accurate measuring utensils transformed baking. Sugar was more affordable, largely as a result of the exploitation of slave labour. People travelled, learned about new dishes and took that knowledge back home. Others emigrated and took their favourite recipes to new lands.

These and other changes resulted in a proliferation of sweet dishes. Professional kitchens made a distinction between cooks and dessert cooks. The French divided the labour between the main kitchen, the cuisine, and the cold kitchen, known as the *office*, where pastries, cakes, custards and ice creams were made. Sweet dishes no longer shared the table; they had their own course, their own chefs, their own tableware and their own menus. Dessert had arrived.

In 1708, more than a century after Vaughan called dessert 'unnatural', William King, author of *The Art of Cookery: A Poem in Imitation of Horace's Art of Poetry*, was inspired to write ''Tis the Dessert that graces all the Feast'. In 1846, Eugene Briffault wrote similarly in *Paris à table*,

> The dessert crowns the dinner. To create a fine dessert, one has
> to combine the skills of a confectioner, a decorator, a painter,
> an architect, an ice-cream maker, a sculptor, and a florist.
> The splendor of such creations appeals above all to the eye –
> the real gourmand admires them without touching them!

I agree with Briffault that the dessert crowns the dinner. However, I do strongly believe that it should be eaten and enjoyed.

Carducius P. Ream's delectable 1861 print is titled simply *Dessert No. 4*.

An 18th-century Dutch still-life of the style called 'little banquet pieces'.

ONE

OUR ANCIENT EATING HABITS

I MAGINE YOU ARE a guest at a festive midwinter dinner. After the main course, while the table is being cleared, your hostess suggests that everyone move to the living room for afters. It is a cold, snowy night and she has prepared a special treat – mulled wine, aromatic with spicy cinnamon, cloves and orange zest. A bowl of sugar-glazed walnuts sits on the coffee table along with a platter of the crisp, waffle-like Italian cookies called *pizzelle*. The highlight of the course is poached pears sprinkled with pomegranate seeds. It is a perfect ending to a winter's evening. Just as it was in the Middle Ages.

At that time, after moving to a different room, the company would enjoy nearly the same food and drink as we do today. The wine was called hippocras and was flavoured with many of the same warm spices we now use in mulled wine, along with some less familiar ones, such as galangal and grains of paradise. The sweetened nuts were called comfits – nuts, seeds or spices coated with sugar. The crisp cookies we know as *pizzelle* or butter wafers were known as wafers, *cialde*, *oublies*, *wafels* or *gaufres*, and they were ubiquitous. Poached pears or other cooked or dried fruits were often served at the conclusion of a meal in medieval times, just as they are today.

The main difference between our festive finale and that of medieval societies is that we think of it as dessert – a course of sweet dishes and drinks separate from the preceding savoury foods of dinner. This was not a medieval concept. These foods were not served because they were sweet, but because they were considered good for digestion. Some were thought to have aphrodisiac qualities, which made them good bedtime snacks. Our reason for enjoying them has changed, but the drinks and dishes themselves have remained surprisingly consistent over the centuries.

During the Middle Ages, throughout Europe, the wealthy ate similar foods in a similar style, but they did not eat dessert. Which is not to say that they did not have sweet dishes; they did. However, sweet dishes were served throughout the meal as well as at its conclusion. Sweet and savoury dishes sat side by side on the table. The idea that one should keep them separate was, literally, unheard of. Dinner in aristocratic households was comprised of a series of courses or servings, each of which consisted of several different dishes all placed on the table at once, rather like exceedingly lavish buffets. Roast venison, rabbits and capons might share the table with almond creams, pudding of swans' necks, a beef stew or potage and meat pies. After these dishes were cleared, another similar serving would be presented. Depending on the household and the occasion, there might be two, three or more servings. When dinner did conclude with sweets such as wafers, fruits or comfits, it was not with the intention of separating the sweet dishes from the rest of the meal. Medical theory was one of the determining factors in dining, at least for the upper classes.

HOUSEHOLD MANAGEMENT

We know a lot about the way they ate, thanks particularly to a book called *Le Ménagier de Paris*, written in the late fourteenth century as a guide to running a bourgeois Parisian *ménage*, or household. It was first translated into English in 1928 by the historian Eileen Power, who titled it *The Goodman of Paris*. The book's author has been the subject of much speculation, but whoever he was, he left us an informative guidebook to his time and place. The book included menus, recipes, lists of supplies and their costs, and notes regarding what should be purchased and what should be prepared within the household.

The author was well into middle age when he married a woman of high social rank who was just fifteen years old. He wrote that he wished the book to help his young wife learn how to administer their household, buy supplies, supervise servants and generally manage their affairs. However, he explained, the point of the book was only in part that she would learn how to manage the household successfully. He had another rather unusual motive as well. He foresaw that he would die before his young wife, and she would inevitably remarry. He wanted to ensure that her household skills would reflect well on him in the eyes of her second husband.

In so doing, the author of the *Ménagier* gave us a window into the world of an affluent medieval French household. Introducing the menus, he wrote:

> Hereafter follow divers dinners and suppers of great lords and others and notes, whereupon you may choose, collect and learn whatsoever dishes it shall please you, according to the seasons and to the meats which are native to the place where you may be, when you have to give a dinner or a supper.[1]

The author listed many menus, usually noting whether they were for fish days or meat days, according to the complex religious rules of the time. Most menus consisted of at least three courses or services, each of which included half a dozen dishes or more.

However, at such dinners, no one tasted every dish. The amount and variety allowed guests to choose those dishes that were most appealing, best met their needs or were close enough so that their servants, who hovered behind them, could make sure they were served. Leftover meats would be turned into pies or hashes. Servants could eat the food that was left on the dishes when they were returned to the kitchen, and other scraps might be distributed to the poor.

Many of the *Ménagier* menus included both sweet and savoury dishes in the same service. Sugared flans, sweet custard tarts, aspics and blancmange made with chicken or capon and decorated with coloured comfits shared the second-course table alongside freshwater fish or 'the best roast that may be had'. Savoury meat, fish and other dishes were often sprinkled with sweet spices, comfits and sugar. The *Ménagier* concluded the recipe for one chicken dish by writing, 'When you have served it forth, powder thereon a spice that is hight [called] red coriander and set pomegranate seeds with comfits and fried almonds round the edge of each bowl.' A menu for a Lenten fish dinner began with roasted apples and Provençal figs roasted with bay leaves, along with pea soup, salted eels and white herring. Most of the menus labelled each course with its number, but occasionally the terms 'dessert', 'issue' and *boute-hors* were used. One final course called 'dessert' included a fruit compote decorated with white and red comfits, flawns (flans), figs, dates, raisins, filberts and rissoles. Typically rissoles were croquettes made with meat, but in this instance, for a fish day, they were made with chestnuts.[2]

The style of eating described in *Le Ménagier de Paris* was similar to the style employed in England as well. In their 1985 book *Curye on Inglysch: English Culinary Manuscripts of the Fourteenth Century (Including The Forme of Cury)*, Constance B. Hieatt and Sharon Butler collected and annotated menus and recipes from more than twenty English manuscripts of the same era. (The word *curye* in the title has nothing to do with the Indian spice blend. It is an old English spelling of 'cooking' or 'cookery'.) The authors pointed out that although the English manuscripts included a few dishes that did not occur in French sources, there were many more similarities than differences. Hieatt and Butler described foods and an order of service that are nearly identical to those described in the *Ménagier*.

Meals followed the culinary logic and medical philosophy of the time, which was not as random as it seems. The system was carried out in accordance with the theories of the ancients – Aristotle,

Hippocrates, Avicenna and Galen – known as the humoral system. According to the theory, humans were thought to contain varying degrees of four humours or fluids – black bile, yellow or red bile, blood and phlegm. The make-up of humours in an individual resulted in their being categorized as either choleric, phlegmatic, melancholy or sanguine. Each quality had its own characteristics and each needed to be balanced to achieve the ideal, which was considered to be a warm, moist body. Foods were selected for their efficacy in balancing the humours. For example, a choleric person was likely hot and dry, so would require cooling and moistening foods, such as lettuce. Sugar was categorized as warm and dry, so it would be used to temper foods and individuals that were cold and moist. That might mean stirring some sugar into a sauce or mixing it with other warm spices and sprinkling it over a dish such as a savoury pottage. Being out of balance would result in disease.

The season also influenced the choice of foods. Hippocras was a cool weather drink. It was not drunk in summer. We still think of ginger, pepper and cinnamon as warm spices and, consciously or not, we are likely to use more of them in winter than in summer. In addition, substantial foods were supposed to be served first, with more delicate foods served later in the meal. That is one of the reasons why such foods as small game birds, fritters and tarts made with fish or meat were served alongside light sweet dishes.

In addition to health and digestion considerations, a medieval host had to bear in mind the status of his guests. Higher-ranking individuals had to be served the choicest foods and the largest portions. Lesser individuals received smaller portions or less desirable foods. Labourers were thought to be able to digest large quantities of coarse foods, but refined nobles were believed to have more delicate constitutions. The religious calendar was also important. Meat was forbidden on Fridays and Saturdays, some Wednesdays, a variety of holy days and throughout Lent; fish, therefore, was served frequently. It was not a simple system. Human nature being what it is, it is likely that few people followed all the rules faithfully.

Banqueting scene from the beautifully illustrated 15th-century book
Les Très riches heures du Duc de Berry.

SPOONSFUL OF SUGAR

Honey was used to sweeten drinks and preserve fruits during the Middle Ages. But honey has a distinctive flavour – it may enhance a dish, but it can also overwhelm other flavours. Sugar, specifically refined white sugar, has no taste of its own apart from pure sweetness. That makes it much more versatile. It was also more costly than honey and, accordingly, more desirable. Sugar travelled a long and circuitous route from its origins to its arrival on medieval European tables. The cultivation of sugar cane and the technology that refined it into sugar journeyed from India to Persia, the Middle East, North Africa and the Mediterranean, before sugar itself finally reached northern Europe. Trade routes, conquests, crusades and written accounts both culinary and medicinal all played a role in spreading the use of the sweet spice. Before the settlement of the New World and the establishment of sugar plantations, at a time when sugar was rare and expensive, even members of the top tier of European society had little. Sugar was a spice, a medicine, to be kept locked in the spice cabinet, used with discretion, but flaunted whenever possible.

Long before Europeans had access to sugar, Middle Eastern cooks used it to sweeten the drinks they called sherbets and to make jams and jellies. They blended sugar with almonds to create marzipan, soaked cakes in sweet syrups made fragrant with roses or orange blossoms, and produced medicinal sugared spices. The Muslim conquest of the Iberian Peninsula and Sicily brought sugar and eastern sweets to those countries and eventually well beyond them. In time, the sweets of the Islamic world would find their way to the convents of Spain, Portugal and Italy and later accompany missionaries and explorers on their travels throughout the world.

As Europeans learned from Middle Eastern culinary practices and trade increased, sugar became more prevalent in European dishes, initially as medicines. Arabic medical texts were translated and spread throughout Europe. Sugar, also known as 'Arab salt' because it had arrived via Arabian countries, was considered good for stomach ailments. It was also prescribed for fevers, coughs, problems of the bladder or kidneys, and even the plague. If it also tasted good, so much the better. In the thirteenth century, the Italian priest and philosopher Thomas Aquinas argued that sugared spices did not break a fast because they were eaten not for nourishment but, according to historian Rachel Laudan, for 'ease in digestion'.[3] This was an important pronouncement, because it gave sugar medical respectability in the Christian world, and it helped pave the way for the controversial sixteenth-century ruling by Pope Gregory XIII that drinking chocolate did not break the religious fast.

Sugar was considered such a necessity that for centuries a common adage described desperate circumstances as being 'like an apothecary without sugar'. Of course, sugar and spices were necessities

From chopping cane to boiling sugar to unmoulding loaves, sugar production in the 16th century was a laborious process.

only for the wealthy. Less affluent people did not have the wherewithal to buy or cook with them, although they sometimes found less expensive alternatives. For the most part, though, ordinary people had to be concerned with filling their stomachs, not balancing their humours.

In the sixteenth and seventeenth centuries, some members of the medical establishment became as negative about sugar as earlier users had been positive. The German physician Hieronymus Bock wrote, in 1539, that sugar was 'an extravagance for the rich', rather than a remedy.[4] When new medical theories gradually began to replace humoral beliefs in the eighteenth century, some doctors decided that sugar caused, rather than cured, many medical problems. Nevertheless, the exploitation of slave labour in European colonies in the New World made sugar a cheap commodity. Consumption among all classes increased substantially, particularly in England, where consumption rose from 3.5 kg (8 lb) per person in 1720 to 6 kg (13 lb) by the end of the century.[5]

SWEET OR SAVOURY?

TO MAKE A TART OF GOOSEBERRIES.
Take Goseberries, and perboyle them in white Claret wine, or Strong Ale, and withall boyle a little white bread: then take them up & draw them through a strainer as thicke as you can with the yolkes of five eggs, then season it up with Sugar, and halfe a dish of Butter, and so bake it.[6]

Many menus from the medieval and Renaissance eras list dishes we think of as desserts, but words can be deceiving. Cooks often used yeast to make cakes rise so that they were more bread-like than cake-like. Custards, pies, tarts, puddings and other such dishes were often savoury, made with meats or fish, rather than the sweet dishes familiar to us. They were made differently as well. We like piecrusts that are flaky and light. In England, piecrusts, which they called 'coffins', were sturdy, freestanding containers for meaty mixtures. Some cooks called for the coffins to be hardened in the oven before filling and baking. They were so durable that the filling could be scooped out and eaten at one meal, and the pie shell refilled with a different filling for another meal. As late as the seventeenth century, coffins were described as being made of 'good, tough wheate paste'.[7]

The gooseberry tart above was sweet, but it might have been served at any time during the meal. It was preceded in the book by a recipe for 'A Tarte to provoke courage either in man or Woman', which called for sparrows as well as dates, quinces and sugar.[8] The tart recipes were followed by recipes for roasted meats. In a fifteenth-century treatise known as *Du Fait de cuisine*, Maistre Chiquart, the cook for the Duke of Savoy, described the making of almond-milk flans. They were sweet flans prepared with almonds, starch, saffron, salt and sugar. But they were served as part of the dinner, not as a sweet or dessert course. Chiquart said that after the custard was cooked, the pastry cook was to make pie shells, bake them firm and then fill them. His directions are an early example of the division of labour between cook and pastry cook. Chiquart recommended a separate pastry kitchen for baking meat and fish pies, flans, custards and tarts.[9] Custards and custard pies could be sweet or savoury, sugared or spiced, or sprinkled

This decorative 16th-century pearwood rolling pin from Germany is incised with religious symbols. Thought to have been used in a pious Protestant household, it allowed the baker to roll and decorate a piecrust at the same time.

Hidden under the crisp, caramelized crust of crème brûlée is a rich creamy custard.

with pepper. Some were made from the same basic mixture we know today, of cream, sugar and eggs, topped with sugar and then toasted under a hot iron to make what was called 'burnt cream'. We would call them crèmes brûlées. Many custards had cheese, meats and fish such as eels or crawfish added, making them more like today's quiches.

Puddings date back at least to the thirteenth century, but they, too, favoured meat over sweet foods, and were served early in the course of the meal. In England, it was common to cook a pudding inside an animal's belly. The sixteenth-century author of *The Good Huswifes Jewell*, Thomas Dawson, cooked this pudding in a veal breast:

TO MAKE A PUDDING IN A BREAST OF VEALE
Take Peresely [parsley], Time [thyme], washe them, pricke them, and choppe them small, then take viii yolkes of egges, grated bread and halfe a pint of creame being verie sweete, then season it with

Pepper, Cloves, and Mace, Saffron, and Sugar, small raisins and salt, put it in and Roste it and serve it.[10]

It was not until the seventeenth century and the introduction of pudding cloths and pudding basins that puddings became sweeter, and present-day favourites such as plum pudding came into being.

Jellies, or *gelées*, appeared frequently on medieval tables, but they were not the highly sweetened (or instant) gelatines we know today. These ancient jellies were high-status luxury dishes. Medieval cooks used ingredients such as deer antlers, ivory dust, pig's trotters (feet) or isinglass (gelatine obtained from fish bladders) to make them set firmly, and often served them atop meat, poultry or fish as a first- or second-course dish. We would call them aspic, brawn or headcheese rather than jelly, with its sugary connotation. Like today's gelatines, however, medieval ones lent themselves to decoration and colouring. Appropriate dyes could be purchased from a 'spicer' (another term for an apothecary), if not made by the cook. Jellies were often moulded and decorated with coats of arms or other emblems to honour a guest, or with a phrase praising God or celebrating an occasion. The cook traced the design on the jelly with a feather dipped into the white of an egg, and then coloured it using a brush dipped in gold or silver.

BY ANY NAME

It would be centuries before a separate course of sweet dishes was served after the main part of the meal and called 'dessert'. Until the nineteenth century, the word was simply used to mean dishes that were served after the previous ones had been cleared. In one fourteenth-century book, a serving of venison and frumenty, a boiled wheat porridge, was called 'dessert'.

The terms used to describe the final course of a dinner were varied, but most implied leave-taking. The sense of leaving was appro-priate, not only because the meal was ending but because the final dishes were often served in another chamber after the guests got up from the table, washed their hands and said grace. Among the terms was *issue de table*, which suggested leaving the table. Another was *boute-hors*, also spelled *boutehors*, from *bouter dehors* meaning 'to push out' – a rather inelegant way to suggest leave-taking. The Anglo-Norman word *voidée* was also used. It probably derived from *voider*, meaning 'to empty out', and referred to withdrawing from a hall or a chamber. In English, 'sally-forth' was much used. A sally port is a controlled entryway, originally in a castle, later in military facilities. 'Sally-forth' means to set out, to go forth. The sally-forth was the last course you ate before you sallied forth home or, if you were the host, to bed.

Today, rather than 'dessert', the term 'afters' is often used in England. It seems quite contemporary, but the term 'after-course' dates back to the fifteenth century, and was probably the genesis of 'afters'. The British often use 'pudding' as a generic word for dessert, whether the dish being served is apple pie, chocolate cake or an actual pudding. In the early part of the twentieth century, 'pudding' was considered a less prestigious term than the French-derived word 'dessert'. According to young Augustus in the English author Kate Atkinson's novel *Life After Life* (2013), pudding was what they had when it was just family. When there were guests, it was dessert.[11] More recently, some English writers have preferred the word 'pudding' for the sweet course, and insist that the fruit course – and only the fruit course – be called 'dessert'. The French culinary historian Jean-Louis Flandrin wrote that in the eighteenth century *fruit* was the aristocratic term for the dessert course, and *dessert* the term of the bourgeoisie. But in the nineteenth century, when the word *fruit* was used, it was written in the plural to indicate that fruits were being served. It was no longer the term for the dessert course.[12]

THE FRUIT

Fruits were among the earliest and most prominent end-of-meal foods throughout Europe and in many other parts of the world. Traditional meals in China, India and Japan typically ended with fruit rather than with a sweet course. In many countries, this has not changed. Dictionaries in French and in English *usually* mention fruit first when defining dessert. The *Oxford English Dictionary* calls dessert 'a course of fruit, sweetmeats, etc. served after a dinner or supper'. The fifteenth-century English historian Raphael Holinshed, writing in *Chronicles of England,* described a cardinal who had not finished dining as 'being then in his fruits'. Ephraim Chamber's *Cyclopedia* of 1741 defined dessert as 'The last Service being brought on the Tables of People of Quality; when the Meats are all taken off. The Dessert consists of Fruits, Pastry-Works, Confections, &c.'[13]

Fruit is a bounteous dessert in this 19th-century American print by Currier & Ives.

Since humoral theory held that raw fruits were cold, dry and dangerous, and the ideal body should be warm and moist, it is interesting that fruits were so important as a last course. People accommodated the problem in various ways. Some held that as long as the fruits were dried or cooked, they were safe to consume. Some recommended drinking wine along with fruits to help counteract their deleterious effects. Others suggested that it would be even better if the fruits were cooked in the wine. Warm spices such as cinnamon, anise and ginger added to the positive force of the wine. Since most fruits, along with foods such as aged cheeses, were thought to relax or close the stomach, according to the unappetizing-sounding principle of the ancients, they were best eaten at the end of a meal. Thus meals concluded with dried fruits, such as dates and raisins, and cooked fruits, such as poached pears and baked apples, along with warming spices, wine and stomach-sealing cheese.

The twelfth-century English scholar Alexander Neckam wrote that because pears were considered cold and injurious, they should be cooked in wine and consumed at the close of a meal. In addition, he believed that because walnuts were categorized among the dangerous herbs or fungi, they should be served with pears to overcome their poison. The thirteenth-century physician Aldobrandino of Siena believed that one should eat pears at the end of a meal to relax the stomach and help with digestion. The final course in one of the meals described in John Russell's fifteenth-century *Book of Nurture* was called a 'Course of Fruit'. It lists hot apples and pears with sugar candy, along with ginger, wafers and hippocras.

Centuries after the humoral doctrine was forgotten, many of its ideas continued to resonate in practice and folklore. In *Cheese, Pears, and History in a Proverb*, author Massimo Montanari quotes the early Italian phrase *aspettare le pere guaste* (to wait for the taste of the pears), and explains that it means to stay at the table until the very end.[14] The French phrase *entre la poire et le fromage, chacun dit sa chanson à boire* – 'between the pear and the cheese, everyone sings his drinking song' – refers to the end of a meal when pears and cheese, as well as more wine, were served, and everyone relaxed.[15]

Along with fruits, cheese, comfits and hippocras, sweetened and spiced quince preserves were also served at the close of medieval dinners. Variously flavoured with red wine, cinnamon and/or ginger, quince paste was made by the ancient Greeks and Romans and sweetened with honey. Medieval Arab confectioners, and later the Spanish and Portuguese, sweetened it with sugar. The Spanish named it *membrillo*, for their word for quince. The Portuguese called it *marmelada*, from *marmelo*, their word for quince. It was the forerunner of today's marmalades. In northern Europe, similar versions were called *chardequince*, *condoignac*, *cotignac* or *quiddony*. The first shipments of *marmelada*, packed in wooden boxes, were imported to London from Portugal in the fifteenth century. Its reputed medical and aphrodisiac powers along with its extraordinarily high cost made it a popular gift among the elite.[16] Today, quince paste and cheese are a popular dessert pairing.

Some fruits, by way of contrast, were thought to help open the stomach and were supposed to be eaten at the beginning of the meal. A fifteenth-century Italian physician, Lorenzo Sassoli, believed that figs, grapes, ripe cherries and melons should be eaten only at the start of the meal. Was this the origin of the Italian antipasto melon and prosciutto?

Many years later, the dangers of fresh fruits forgotten, the finest ones were prized. Alexandre Dumas, in his *Grand Dictionnaire de cuisine*, told the story of a man named Giradot who had a request to make to King Louis XIV. It is not clear what the request was, but possibly it was for a pension, since that is what he received. A former musketeer, Giradot had retired to a village near Montreuil, east of Paris, and devoted himself to gardening. His peaches were magnificent, according to Dumas, and he sent a dozen to the king along with the message 'For the king's dessert'. Impressed, the king himself went to see the garden and thank the gardener who had produced such fruit. As a result, Giradot received a pension and the honour of supplying

A *fraisier* combines strawberries with sponge cake and cream to create a stunning dessert.

a basket of his most beautiful peaches every year for the king's table. The family kept up the tradition until the Revolution.[17]

Even now, in many cultures, dessert is likely to be fruit. Pastries and the like are saved for special occasions or enjoyed as afternoon snacks. *The Anatomy of Dessert*, written in 1929, was not about tarts, cakes or puddings. Author Edward Bunyard, an English nurseryman, was writing about the delights of fresh fruits and the wines that best accompanied them. Mireille Johnston, author of *The Cuisine of the Sun*, was born, fittingly, in an apricot-coloured house overlooking the sea in Nice. She wrote that the *Niçois* word for dessert was *la frucha*, the fruit, and that most of the time the fruit served came from the family orchard. 'Fresh, stewed, dried, confit, or kept in brandy', fruits are family desserts rather than the 'elaborate cream-rich desserts of haute cuisine', she explained.[18] She was writing in, and describing, the 1970s.

Unleavened Bread

Along with fruit, a final serving of wafers and hippocras is omnipresent in medieval sources. Its religious echo of bread and wine was not coincidental. Wafers had their origins in Jewish *matzah*, the unleavened bread of Passover, and the Communion wafers used in the Catholic Mass. They were called *obleyes* or *oublies*, from the Latin *oblate*, or 'offering'. Like their religious predecessors, secular wafers were made from a batter cooked between two irons. The wafer-maker poured the batter onto the greased and preheated iron, squeezed the two halves together by means of their handles and held them over the heat source. When the wafer was cooked on one side, the maker turned the iron over to cook it on the other side. The irons were made with long handles to protect the wafer-maker from the heat. Wafers are pliable before they cool and were often rolled into cylinders or cone shapes to crisp up, as can be seen in illustrated manuscripts and paintings of the period.

The irons used to make religious wafers were forged with religious designs; those used for secular wafers featured designs such as coats of arms or honeycombs. The honeycomb design probably led to them being called *wafel* in German, from the old High German word for honeycomb, *wabe*. In France, they were called *gaufre* or *gauffrette* (written as *gofer* in some later English books), words also derived from honeycomb.

The batter for some early wafers was sweetened with honey, but by the fourteenth century most recipes called for sugar. The other ingredients were flour, eggs, milk or cream, and often a spice such as nutmeg or

This 15th-century wafer iron from Umbria was likely used to make wafers for a wedding. Its inscription is translated as 'Service is never lost and a perfect love is ever more green.'

ginger. One of the *Ménagier*'s recipes recommended topping the batter with a slice of cheese, then adding more batter and finally cooking it. In this way, the author wrote, 'the cheese remaineth between the two pastes and is thus set between two irons'.[19] It sounds rather like our grilled-cheese sandwich or cheese toastie.

Making wafers was the province of waferers, rather than cooks, and by the twelfth century a wafer-makers' guild had been formed in France. In Tudor England, wafers were a delicacy reserved for king and court or for special feast days. Royal as well as other wealthy households employed their own waferers. Wafers could be purchased, and although the *Ménagier* offered recipes, it also noted that for a wedding feast the author bought them from a waferer.

In Paris, wafer-makers made and sold their wares on the streets, often setting up in front of churches on feast days or selling from stalls at fairs. They rolled the wafers into cones and tucked them inside each other, selling five as a *main d'oublies*. Both men and women sold wafers in Paris and, since they were considered to be discreet, they were trusted to pass clandestine notes to lovers, along with the *oublies*, without arousing the suspicion of spouses. Sellers also rolled dice with their customers to allow them to try to win rather than buy wafers. One of the street cries they created to attract business was '*Voilà le plaisir, mesdames!*' (Here's pleasure, ladies!), and so in addition to *oublies* and *gaufres*, wafers also became known as *plaisirs*.

Wafers continue to live on today under a variety of names. The Germans bake a cookie called *Lebkuchen* atop a thin white wheat wafer called an *Oblaten*, which resembles a Communion wafer. Dutch wafer cookies are called *Stroopwafels* and are usually sweetened with honey. The Italian word meaning wafer is *cialde*. However, *pizzelle* are wafers made the same way as *gaufres* and *oublies*. In John Florio's 1611 edition of *Queen Anna's New World of Words, or Dictionarie of the Italian and English Tongues*, his definition of

The pleasures of wafers and wine in a 17th-century painting by Lubin Baugi.

pizza includes 'a wafer. Also a kind of sugar tart'.[20] The diminutive *pizzelle* is used in the Abruzzo region, where they are still made and celebrated at festivals. Immigrants brought them to the u.s., Canada, Australia and other countries, where they became a popular snack biscuit as well as a dessert. In English-speaking countries, wafers have been called cornets, cornucopias and cones. Eventually they became ice-cream cones.

MEDICINAL WINE

In the Middle Ages, the spiced wine hippocras – also spelled hypocras, ypocras and ipocras – generally accompanied wafers. Named after Hippocrates, the ancient Greek physician and father of medicine, the drink dates to the early medieval period. Although Hippocrates did not invent or drink it, its name is derived from the Old French word for the physician, *ypocrate* – in Middle English, *ipocras*. From the fourteenth century until the eighteenth, doctors prescribed *vinum Hippocraticum*, the wine of Hippocrates, for digestive as well as other ailments.

Hippocras was referred to as a warm drink because it was made with spices that humoral theory considered warm and moist, perfect to help balance the humours of a cold, dry person, or to enjoy on a chill winter's night. Unlike today's mulled wines, hippocras does not seem to have been heated. In addition to sugar (or honey), it could include such spices as cinnamon, cloves, ginger, grains of paradise and musk. In a summer menu, the author of the *Ménagier* wrote that hippocras was not served because it was not appropriate to the season. With all of its warm spices, hippocras was a winter drink.

Hippocras was made of either white or red wine. Some recipes specified one or the other, while some simply called for wine. The spices and sugar were steeped in the wine, usually overnight so that the wine would absorb all the sweet spicy flavour. Then the wine was strained through a conical bag made of sturdy cotton, linen, flannel or wool. The bag was called Hippocrates' sleeve, although it resembles the sleeve of a medieval noble's gown rather than a Greek toga. Some cooks added milk to the mixture – not to make a milky drink, but because the milk would form curds when it came into contact with the acidic wine. The curds and spices would then separate from the wine, leaving a clear liquid. It was usually strained two or three times to make the wine perfectly clear, whether white or red. Today, bartenders are reintroducing the process, which they call 'milk-washing', to clarify cocktails.

The spice mixture was not discarded after the hippocras had been strained, but saved to flavour stews or pottages. Each apothecary, cook, or master or mistress of a household had his or her own preferred spice mixture. One could also buy a prepared hippocras spice mixture from an apothecary or spicer, or even buy ready-made hippocras.

The best rationalization for drinking hippocras came from Samuel Pepys, an English member of parliament in the seventeenth century. Well known today for his diaries of everyday life in Restoration England, he wrote on 29 October 1663,

> We went into the Buttery . . . and there wine was offered and they drunk, I only drinking some hypocras, which doth not break my vowe, it being, to the best of my present judgement, only a mixed compound drink, and not any wine. If I am mistaken, God forgive me! But I hope and do think I am not.[21]

By the eighteenth century, hippocras had largely fallen out of favour, though similarly spiced wines continued to be popular, especially in northern European countries, and particularly in wintertime. James Boswell, the Scottish biographer and friend of Samuel Johnson, wrote in his diary on 19 January 1763 that he went into a public house and drank 'some warm white wine with aromatic spices, pepper and cinnamon'.[22]

ALL HAIL KISSING COMFITS

After the wafers and hippocras were served and the meal was drawing to a conclusion, comfits might be served. Also known as chamber spices, kissing comfits, confetti, dragées, Jordan almonds, bonbons and sugarplums, these were and are sugar-coated nuts, dried fruits or spices. In medieval times, because they were considered to have medicinal merit, they were sprinkled on savoury as well as sweet foods, mixed into cakes and drinks, served at the conclusion of festive meals, eaten as bedtime snacks and presented as gifts to favoured recipients.

The *Oxford English Dictionary* definition of 'comfit' is 'a sweetmeat made of some fruit, root, etc., preserved with sugar; now usually a small round or oval mass of sugar enclosing a caraway seed, almond, etc.; a sugar-plum'. The word derives from the Latin verb *conficere*, meaning to prepare, make ready. Confect, confection, confectioner – these are just some of the words we have derived from *conficere*. The word 'comfit' came to be used in English. *Confetto* or, more commonly, the plural *confetti* is used in Italian. The French, however, adopted the word *dragée* to describe a sugar-coated seed or nut. The word, like 'dredge' (meaning to coat with an ingredient such as flour or sugar), seems to have been derived from the Latin *tragēmata*, according to the *OED*.

The cost of sugar, as well as the specialized equipment and skills required to make comfits, meant they were a rich person's remedy, usually bought from an apothecary. The definition of dragée from the *OED* is 'a sugarplum or sweetmeat in the centre of which is a drug; intended for the more pleasant administration of medicinal substances. In modern use not restricted to sweetmeats serving as a vehicle for drugs; often a sugared almond.' Comfits, confetti, dragées – they were the original sugar-coated pills. In medieval times, the sugar coating might have concealed chopped ginger or coriander, anise, caraway, fennel or celery seeds. Or the comfits might have been sugar-coated almonds, pistachios, filberts, the kernels of

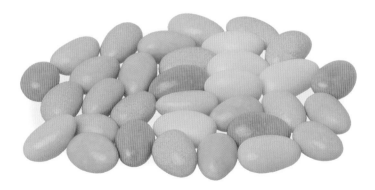

Today's pretty pastel jordan almonds make a colourful addition to the dessert course.

apricots or cherries, or slivers of cinnamon. Roots including angelica and iris, or orris, were dried and ground into powder, and then combined with sugar and gum arabic to make a paste. The paste was rolled into tiny balls and then candied to make comfits.

By the fifteenth century, royal confectioners were making comfits for kings, queens and nobles. Comfits were usually eaten after dinner while standing up, to help the elite digest their substantial meals without discomfort. In addition to their aphrodisiac qualities, caraway and fennel seed comfits were used to sweeten breath, which is why Falstaff in the *Merry Wives of Windsor* calls for the sky to 'hail kissing-comfits' (Act v, scene 5). The word 'comfit' is pronounced more like 'comfort' than 'comfee', and caraway comfits were among the most popular. As a result, Thomas Heywood was able to make these puns in his seventeenth-century play *The Fair Maid of the West*: 'I will make bold to march in towards your banquet, and there comfit me selfe, and cast all carawayes downe my throat.'[23]

The *Ménagier* listed 3 lb (1.5 kg) of white comfits for the sally-forth of a wedding dinner. On another festive occasion, the author purchased red comfits to sprinkle atop a blancmange along with pomegranate seeds, rather than to serve at the end of the meal. It was noted that the comfits were to be purchased from a spicer rather than prepared in the household. Making comfits was a difficult task best left to professionals. Over the years equipment improved, but basically one put the seeds or nuts into a basin, held it over a heat source until the ingredients were heated through, then poured previously melted sugar (as a syrup) over them and swirled it around to cover them. The apothecary had to rub the hot syrup over the seeds by hand to make sure each one was coated with sugar, and that they did not stick to each other or to the pan. They would be allowed to dry, and then the process would be repeated, sometimes several times over the course of three or four days.

By the seventeenth century, cooks and confectioners were more apt to make comfits than were apothecaries, but the process had not become easier. Hannah Woolley, the first female author of a printed cookbook in English, described the process in detail in the 1684 edition of *The Queene-like Closet or Rich Cabinet: Stored with All Manner of Rare Receipts For Preserving, Candying and Cookery. Very Pleasant and Beneficial to all Ingenious Persons of the Female Sex.* After describing the equipment that was to be 'in readiness', she wrote:

> Melt your Sugar in this manner, put in three Pounds of Sugar into the Basin, and one Pint of Water, stir it well till it be wet, then melt it very well and boil it very softly until it will stream from the Ladle like Turpentine, and not drop, then let it seeth no more, but keep it upon warm Embers, that it may run from the Ladle upon the seeds.
>
> Move the Seeds in the hanging Basin so fast as you can or may, and with one hand, cast on half a Ladle full at a time of the hot Sugar, and rub the Seeds with your other hand a pretty while, for that will make them take the Sugar the better, and dry them well after every Coat.
>
> Do thus at every Coat, not only in moving the Basin, but also with stirring of the Comfits with the one hand, and drying the same: in every hour you may make three pounds of Comfits; as the Comfits do increase in bigness, so you may take more Sugar in your Ladle to cast on:
>
> But for plain Comfits, let your Sugar be of a light decoction last, and of a high decoction first, and not too hot.

For crisp and ragged Comfits make your decoction so high,
as that it may run from the Ladle, and let it fall a foot high or
more from the Ladle, and the hotter you cast on your sugar, the
more ragged will your Comfits be; also the Comfits will not take
so much of the sugar, as upon a light decoction, and they will
keep their raggedness long; this high decoction must serve for
eight or ten Coats, and put on at every time but one Ladle full.[24]

Not all comfits were smooth. Some were intentionally made
with a bumpy or, as Woolley wrote, ragged texture, which was especially popular at the time. They were not all white either. Some were
tinted red, yellow, blue or green with vegetable colourings during
the final sugar coating. Rose petals were used to colour them red or
pink; saffron turned them to gold; spinach coloured them green;
cornflowers, blue.[25]

Excellent status symbols, comfits were served on elegant, often
bejewelled plates at weddings and other celebrations. They were stored
in luxurious little boxes called *drageoirs*, after the French *dragées*. The

A suitably elegant
17th-century English
comfit container.

contents were not quite as precious as jewels, but the *drageoirs* were as decorative and intricately designed as jewel boxes. Guests in France were often given a *drageoir* or a dainty basket filled with comfits and other sweets to take home at the end of a banquet. Comfits were sometimes called *bon-bons* in France and offered in similarly posh containers called *bonbonnières*. Comfits were also believed to cure infertility, which is why they were presented – and tossed like rice – at weddings.

Comfits were given to visiting dignitaries and church officials. In the city of Verdun in northeastern France, which is known for the quality of its dragées, they were once the official gifts of bishops. In 1575 the people of Verdun gave Henri III a dozen boxes of sugared almonds for his coronation. The city of Sulmona in Italy, also known for the quality of its confetti, has a museum devoted to the sweet. The Museo dell'arte confettiera is located in a remodelled sixteenth-century building that once housed Fabbrica confetti pelino, Sulmona's most famous confetti manufacturer.

At weddings and at carnival time, comfits were tossed the way paper confetti is tossed today. In the *Journal of Sir Walter Scott*, published in 1891, Scott recalls an event where 'Compliments flew about like sugar-plums at an Italian carnival.'[26] To make them in quantity was costly, so some confectioners cut corners. They coated the almonds or seeds with flour before tossing them with sugar syrup. That meant they could build the layers up faster, with less sugar. If a small amount of flour helped speed the process and cut expense, more flour was even better. It was a cheaper, quicker way to make comfits, and they were still edible, though probably not as tasty as the more refined ones. Still another solution was to make ersatz comfits that were not intended to be eaten, but specifically produced to be thrown. These were made of plaster in the shape and size of the candied almonds and sold by the basketful to be hurled at friends, lovers and strangers during carnival parades. Tossing comfits was a flirtation device, a way to get the attention of a prospective beau or belle.

Confetti tossing during carnival time in 19th-century Rome was not for the faint-hearted.

When Goethe was in his late thirties, he spent two years travelling in Italy and wrote about his impressions of the country and its customs in *Italian Journey*, written 1787–8. Goethe called the Roman carnival 'a kind of small war, mostly playful, but often all too serious'. He described masqueraders on foot and in carriages filling the streets, people who watched the spectacle from their balconies and vendors who strolled through the crowds carrying huge baskets full of the plaster pellets to sell to the costumed carousers. The revellers bought pounds of the pellets to arm themselves, filling sacks or tied-up handkerchiefs with them. Some of the women carried theirs in pretty silvered or gilded baskets.

The most irresistible targets, according to Goethe, were the *abbés*, whose black coats were soon spotted with white and grey where the plaster confetti hit them. But everyone came under fire. Men tossed confetti at pretty girls to get their attention. Women surreptitiously tossed their confetti at handsome young men. Before long, carriages and coats, hats and streets all seemed to be covered in snow. It was all great fun, except when it was not. Every now and then, Goethe wrote, a masquerader threw his confetti with too much enthusiasm, hurting the lady he had sought to impress. Her friends defended her by attacking the offender. Only the presence of the police and the spectre of *corde*, or hanging nooses, hung up at several corners, kept the confrontations from becoming too dangerous.[27] For the most part, however, the festivities were playful, the plaster dust was quickly cleaned up, and all was well.

Before long, carnival-goers learned to wear dusters, coats that protected their outfits from the plaster dust. They even equipped themselves with wire masks to protect their eyes from injury, since a plaster pellet in the eye could cause real damage. (Some carnival-goers had begun to use scoops rather like miniature coal shovels to hurl pellets by the scoopful rather than the handful, so these defensive measures became a necessity.) By the time Charles Dickens visited in 1844–5, the small war had escalated dramatically. Although Dickens marvelled at the good humour everyone displayed, as most of the other carnival-goers did, he had his own wire mask to protect himself. He reported in *Pictures from Italy* that even the carriages had dusters. 'All the carriages were open, and had the linings carefully covered with white cotton or calico, to prevent their proper decorations from being spoiled by the incessant pelting,' he explained. He described the mock battle:

> Carriages, delayed long in one place, would begin a deliberate engagement with other carriages, or with people at the lower windows; and the spectators at some upper balcony or window, joining in the fray, and attacking both parties, would empty down great bags of confétti, that descended like a cloud, and in an instant made them white as millers.[28]

Whether it was created in response to the dangers of confetti made with plaster or simply as an innovative product, a new item using the same name made its debut at the end of the nineteenth century. An 1894 advertising poster by Henri de Toulouse-Lautrec depicted a happy, smiling young woman being showered with colourful – and harmless – confetti made from paper. J. & E. Bella, a London stationery company, commissioned the poster.

Paper confetti was a great improvement on plaster confetti. The bits of paper could be tossed with abandon. They were inexpensive, festive and so light that it did not hurt to be hit with a flurry of confetti. Paper confetti did not leave its mark on clothing, so masks and dusters were not required. No wonder the initial newspaper reports were nearly delirious about the new product. On 26 March 1894, the *New York Times* reported that there was a new carpet on the boulevards of Paris: 'The confetti made a velvet soft to the feet, picturesque to the eye, and novel even to the most advanced taste.' Paper confetti reigned at parades, weddings and carnivals. It replaced plaster confetti, and returned comfits, confetti and dragées to their role as sweets rather than projectiles.

Comfits, known by a variety of names, are still served in countries all over the world. In Iran, the New Year begins on the first day of spring and is called *Nowruz*. Traditionally seven sweets are served in celebration, among them comfits called *noghis*, sugar-coated almonds, and *sohan asali*, almonds cooked with honey and saffron and garnished with pistachios. India's sweet *saunf* or *valiary*, England's aniseed balls, France's *Les Anis de Flavigny, un bien bon bonbon*, which, despite the anise in the names, are available in several flavours – all are comfits. They may be children's sweets (Alice had a box of comfits with her on her journey to Wonderland) or adults' breath-fresheners. The comfit that most closely evokes the past is the jordan almond. Named for the French word for garden, *jardin*, not the country, jordan almonds are often presented as a parting gift to wedding guests, much as comfits were given to guests at the close of an elegant medieval dinner. Instead

Henri de Toulouse-Lautrec's 1894 depiction of harmless paper confetti tossing.

The Pelino company in Sulmona, Italy, notes that its confetti is made according to a 300-year-old recipe and never contains flour or other starches.

of a bejewelled *drageoir*, they are tucked into a beribboned tulle bag. They are no longer considered medicine, but are thought to be lucky, especially when offered in groups of five. The number represents health, wealth, happiness, fertility and longevity.

Today, when we drink spicy mulled wine in winter, enjoy slices of quince paste along with our manchego cheese or conclude a meal with pears poached in red wine and sweet spices, we are not trying to close our stomachs or balance our humours, but we are following the ancient prescriptions. Its reason for being has changed, but the last course of a medieval dinner is often our last course as well.

TWO

Eating with Our Eyes

I F WE EAT with our eyes, as the saying goes, elite Europeans ate very well during the Middle Ages. This was the era of fantastic table displays, of turreted castles sculpted from sugar glistening in candlelight, of peacocks brought to the table dressed in their colourful plumage, and roasted boars' heads served spewing fire from their mouths. (A wad of cotton soaked in camphor and alcohol and lit just before serving did the trick.)[1]

In England, the medieval showstoppers were called subtelties, though subtle is the last word we would use to describe them today. At the time, the Anglo-Norman word *subtelity* – also spelled as *sotilté*, *sotelté* or *sotileté* – referred to intricacy or ingenuity in design workmanship, which was an accurate description. In Italy, they were known as *trionfi*, or triumphs. In France, they were called *entremets*, which means between dishes or courses. Served after one set of dishes had been cleared and another was being readied, they filled the time and space on the table and were an opportunity to impress and entertain guests, as well as display power, wealth and skill.

Subtelties, *trionfi*, *entremets* – these could be savoury or sweet. They could be a musical entertainment or a short play known as an interlude, like the entr'acte or brief performance between acts of a play. Some *entremets* presented a political message. For example, one might display models of castles with banners flying to remind guests of their host's vast domain. Made of sugar, pastry or pasteboard, they

On 28 February 1693 this sugar sculpture adorned the banquet table
at the Palazzo Vizzani in Bologna.

depicted anything from a forest scene to a church complete with several altars. Many were edible, but that was not a requirement. It was more important to be visually entertaining and spectacular. Creating such presentations was an enormous, labour-intensive and expensive undertaking. Preparing subtelties for a particularly festive or politically important event gave employment to dozens of craftsmen – carpenters, painters, sculptors – as well as cooks, servers and scullery workers. The event itself might also employ singers, dancers and musicians.

Although only the privileged enjoyed such spectacles at dinner, anyone could enjoy them vicariously through nursery rhymes such as this old English one:

> Little King Boggen, he built a fine hall,
> Pie-crust and pastry-crust, that was the wall;
> The windows were made of black puddings and white,
> And slated with pancakes – you ne'er saw the like!

Ordinary folk could also see fantastic structures made from food at carnivals and outdoor festivals. A seventeenth-century woodcut by Francesco Orilia illustrates a monumental arch made of bread, cheese, fruits, salami and suckling pig. Made in honour of Duke Antonio Alvarez de Toledo, Viceroy of Naples, for the feast of St John the Baptist, it was intended to demonstrate the duke's generosity.[2] Whether built of sugar or sausages, piecrust or butter, *entremets* were impressive. Some were as startling as the one described in this familiar English nursery rhyme:

> Sing a song of sixpence
> A pocket full of rye
> Four and twenty blackbirds baked in a pie
> When the pie was opened the birds began to sing
> Wasn't that a dainty dish to set before the king?

As fanciful as the verse seems, live blackbirds were actually served in a pie. They were not baked, however; instead they were let loose to sing and fly about the room when the pie was opened. To achieve this, a pie's sturdy crust was filled with bran and baked. When it was done, a hole was cut in the bottom of the pie, and the bran was poured out. Then the person in charge of such things would tuck the live birds into the empty pie, replace the opening and have it served forth. At the table, a servant would lift the lid off the pie and the birds would fly out, to the amusement of the guests.

Robert May was a late seventeenth-century English cook and author, but his ideas about food were firmly rooted in earlier times. A royalist who had trained in France, he delighted in spectacle. His book, *The Accomplisht Cook*, was first published in 1660, the year Charles II returned to the throne after the defeat of the Puritan regime of Oliver Cromwell, and what May called 'delights of the Nobility' were again celebrated in England. In addition to more than one thousand recipes for foods that were meant to be eaten, he described fabulous, often inedible – some might say incredible – dishes to set before a king and other important guests.

In a section of his book titled 'Triumphs and Trophies in Cookery, to be used at Festival Times, as Twelfth-day, &c.', May described making a pasteboard ship, complete with flags, streamers and guns for the table. He made a stag, also of pasteboard, and filled it with claret. An arrow was stuck in the stag's side. The ensemble was set on a large platter, surrounded by salt. Eggshells, filled with rosewater after the egg had been blown out, were arranged in the salt. Pies, some filled with frogs and some with birds, were placed on either side. The whole arrangement was then presented to the table, presumably to the 'oohs' and 'aahs' of the guests. May wrote that the ladies would be asked to pull the arrow from the stag, whereupon the wine, looking like blood, would pour out. The pasteboard guns would then go off with puffs of powder. After that, May explained,

Let the Ladies take the eggshells full of sweet water and throw them at each other. All dangers being seemingly over, by that time you may suppose they will desire to see what is in the pyes; where lifting first the lid off one pye, out skip some Frogs, which make the Ladies to skip and shreek; next after the other pye, whence come out the Birds, who by a natural instinct flying in the light, will put out the Candles; so that what with the flying Birds and skipping Frogs, the one above, the other beneath, will cause much delight and pleasure to the whole company: at length the Candles are lighted and a banquet brought in, the Musick sound, and every one with much delight and content rehearses their actions in the former passages.[3]

Long after the practice ended, children delighted in nursery rhymes and comical illustrations featuring blackbirds in pies. The well-known English artist Walter Crane created this image in 1865.

When the pye was open'd,
The birds began to sing,
Was'nt that a dainty dish
To set before the King?

Over time, *entremets* evolved from entertainments to edibles. They ranged from vegetables or egg dishes to creams or cakes, but gradually the sweet dishes won out over the savoury ones. Today's *entremets* seem dull in comparison to those of May's era. Pastry chefs do create impressive spectacles for the dessert table, but skipping frogs and flying birds are no longer considered dining-room entertainment, and tossing water-filled eggshells at one another is not tolerated at most dinners. On restaurant dessert menus today, the word *entremet* is used to mean layer cakes with soft, rich fillings such as mousses or ganaches. They may be embellished with caramel sauces, chocolate glazes, fruit compotes, sweet biscuit crumbles or tuiles, the wafer-thin biscuits (cookies) shaped like roof tiles. In today's pastry and baking competitions, making impressive *entremets* is one of the tests of a pastry chef's skills.

BANQUETS OF SWEETS

The banquet May referred to was a course of sweetmeats that concluded festive dinners. Also spelled *banquette*, the term itself dates back to the sixteenth century. In Scotland, it was called a cake and wine banquet; in northern England, a fruit banquet. Not to be confused with the elaborate, often official, formal meal we think of as a banquet, this was a course of sweets often served in a separate room or building from the main meal. It grew out of the earlier habit of enjoying comfits and hippocras in a separate chamber after dinner. Sweet banquets were designed to impress, and cooks made ever more elaborate dishes. The sweets were still considered medicinal and aids to digestion, however delightful they may have been to eat, but clearly they were a predecessor to the dessert course.

The word 'banquet' was used to refer to the course, the foods served and the buildings that were constructed on grand estates specifically for banqueting. Strolling through an estate's garden after dinner and arriving at a banqueting house to enjoy sweetmeats and wine was

The goddesses Juno and Cybele sculpted from sugar presided over the
Earl of Castlemaine's table on 14 January 1687.

a pleasant diversion. The elegant structures were often built on hills
with views of a lake or a garden. Some were built atop roofs to take
advantage of an especially picturesque vista. People with a Puritanical
turn of mind thought they were lovers' hideaways and disapproved,
but others delighted in them. Henry VIII had a banqueting house
at Hampton Court. Queen Elizabeth's favourite was a three-storey
banqueting house on a hill at her palace at Nonsuch, 16 km (10 miles)
from London.[4] Elizabeth was famed for her love of sweets and the
blackened teeth that were its result. At the time, when a pound of sugar
cost the equivalent of a day's wages for a craftsman, only the wealthy
could indulge in such banquets.

Cookbooks of the era include nearly identical lists 'of all things
necessarie for a banquet' or 'banqueting conceits'. The anonymous
author of *The Closet for Ladies and Gentlewomen*, published in 1611,
titled the section on banqueting foods 'Here beginneth Banqueting

conceits, as marmalades, Quodiniacks [quince and other fruit pastes], and such like.' The recipes include a variety of comfits, jellies, fruit pastes and creams, as well as 'birds and beastes to stand on their legs' moulded from sugar and gilded. The author made a 'Biskatello', a sugar-paste mixture shaped like small loaves of bread, arranged on wafers and baked. The instructions say that when they are done, 'specke them with gold, and so boxe them. It is a very fine banqueting conceit.' A sugar-paste walnut is described that is made so that 'when you cracke it, you shall find Biskets and Carrawayes in it, or a pretty poesie written.' The author states that similar banqueting fancies were 'excellent good to please children'.[5]

The Closet for Ladies and Gentlewomen was written for the nobility, but the idea of a banquet course spread to less affluent households as well. Gervase Markham (1568–1637) was an English poet, playwright and author of works on veterinary medicine, hunting, hawking and riding. He also wrote *The English Housewife*, one of the most important books on English housewifery published in the early seventeenth century. Reissued and revised many times since its first publication, in 1620 it sailed aboard a ship from England to Virginia, making it the first cookbook known to have been sent to the American colonies. These are Markham's instructions for the proper sequence of a banquet:

ORDERING OF BANQUETS

You shall first send forth a dish made for shew onely, as Beast, Bird, Fish, Fowle . . . then your Marchpane, then preserved Fruite, then a Paste, then a wet sucket, then a dry sucket, Marmelade, comfits, apples, peares, wardens [a type of pear], oranges and lemmons sliced; and then waters, and another dish of preserved fruites . . . no two dishes of one kind going or standing together, and this will not onely appeare delicate to the eye, but invite the appetite with the much variety thereof.[6]

Markham wrote for rural housewives and gentlewomen, not for the nobility as had most earlier cookbook writers. However, Markham's housewife was not the spouse of a common labourer. She was a literate, landed, prosperous partner in her household, and she had enormous responsibilities, as the topics in Markham's book make clear. Well organized and thorough, the book includes sections on medicine, cooking, distilling, brewing, baking, dairying, dyeing and banqueting.[7] Markham introduced his section on banqueting dishes by writing that although such 'pretty and curious secrets' were not of general use, they were 'needful for adornation'. A proper housewife, he wrote, should know how to make them. Part of the reason for the housewife having that responsibility was sugar's medicinal role, and her duty to provide medicine for the household. In addition, sugar was still costly, so it was important to keep a watchful eye on it to prevent pilfering. As a result, the lady of the house and her maids usually produced these sweet delicacies. The frontispiece of T. Hall's book *The Queen's Royal Cookery* (1709) depicts male cooks tending meat over a raging fire and female cooks distilling and making pastry. Still today, men are associated with grilling; women with pastry making.

Markham's many recipes for banqueting dishes were not so different from those of the medieval era. They included jellies, marmalades, Banbury cakes, gingerbread, spice cakes, faux cinnamon sticks made from sugar paste, the biscuits called jumbals, a confection made from marzipan known as marchpane and the sweetmeats called suckets, as well as hippocras and other drinks. The following is Markham's recipe for 'jumbals':

> To make the best Jumbals, take the whites of three egges and beate them well, and take off the froth; then take a little milke and a pound of fine wheate flower & sugar together finely sifted, and a few Aniseeds well rub'd and dried, and then worke all together as stiff as you can worke it, and so make them in what forms you please, and bake them in a soft oven upon white Papers.[8]

SUGAR DELIGHTS

The stunning visual displays on banquet tables relied on the ability of confectioners to work with sugar. Confectioners in the Islamic world were skilled in sugarwork at least by the eleventh century, and it is likely that their knowledge was spread through trade between the Middle East and Venice, and then on to European courts. European confectioners learned that sugar could be boiled into a clear syrup, spun into silver threads and cooked down to a deep, rich caramel. During the fifteenth century, again following Middle Eastern practice, they began combining sugar with a Mediterranean shrub's resin called gum tragacanth. The result was sugar paste, also known as sugar plate or pastillage. It transformed table decor. Gum tragacanth, also called gum dragon or dragon, created a strong and malleable bond with sugar and allowed sugar to be shaped by hand or moulded. Sugar sculpture soared to new heights and extraordinary complexity. Castles, knights, camels, elephants, buildings, birds and beasts – often with political, historical or mythological themes – were all sculpted or moulded from sugar paste. The pieces were left white, painted or gilded according to the confectioner's whimsy. They were so extraordinary that the banquet was often known as the sugar banquet.

When Henry of Valois, the king of Poland and soon-to-be Henry III, king of France, visited Venice in 1574, he was entertained lavishly wherever he went. After visiting the Venetian arsenal, where he was impressed by the armaments on display, he was offered a sugar collation. There, he was equally impressed by the artistic creations made from marzipan and sugar paste. But when he sat down to eat and picked up his napkin, he was astonished. It was made from sugar. In fact, everything from the plates to the bread to the cutlery was made of sugar. The next day, he was treated to another sugar banquet consisting of three hundred female figures made of the whitest, purest sugar – a sugar seraglio. One of the figures was a queen offering two crowns to the king. At the end of the banquet, the guests were given

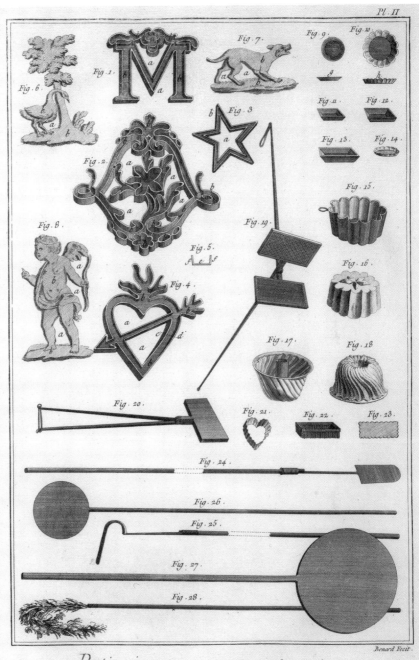

Pl. II

Fig. 1. Fig. 2. Fig. 3. Fig. 4. Fig. 5. Fig. 6. Fig. 7. Fig. 8. Fig. 9. Fig. 10. Fig. 11. Fig. 12. Fig. 13. Fig. 14. Fig. 15. Fig. 16. Fig. 17. Fig. 18. Fig. 19. Fig. 20. Fig. 21. Fig. 22. Fig. 23. Fig. 24. Fig. 25. Fig. 26. Fig. 27. Fig. 28.

Benard Fecit.

Patissier, Tourtieres, Moules, Gaufrier, Pèles &c.

Tools of the 18th-century confectioner's trade.

special bags to carry the sweet creations away with them. As for the king, he was so impressed that he ordered 39 smaller sugar sculptures to take back to France.[9]

Sugar banquets were especially appropriate for weddings. The grand finale of a regal wedding at a Düsseldorf castle in 1585 was particularly extraordinary. As depicted in a print attributed to Frans Hogenberg, a cloth-covered table displays enormous sugar sculptures of castles, trees, fish, lions, an elephant, a man on horseback and more. The towering sugar works dwarf the guests in the foreground of the print. As soon as the wedding festival concluded, guests broke the sculptures into pieces and claimed them as souvenirs.[10]

Allowing guests or even spectators to smash and eat the decor was typical. John Evelyn, who later became famous for writing *Acetaria: A Discourse of Sallets*, an early book on salads, also wrote in diaries, letters and other papers about the many dinners he attended. In an entry for December 1685, he described a banquet given by James II for Venetian ambassadors:

> The banquet was twelve vast chargers piled up so high that those that sat one against another could hardly see each other. Of these sweetmeats, which doubtless took some days piling up in this exquisite manner, the Ambassadors touched not, but leaving them to the spectators who came out of curiosity to see the dinner, were exceedingly pleased to see in what a moment of time all that curious work was demolished, the comfitures voided, and the tables cleared.[11]

During the Ottoman period, Turkish confectioners were famed for their sweets. Like their European counterparts, they made elaborate sugar decor for royal and religious occasions, particularly circumcisions and weddings. They created sugar gardens, animals, backgammon and chess sets, and figures from mythology. Gardens were a speciality. Sugar tulips, roses and jonquils blossomed in flowerbeds made of brown sugar soil. Garden pathways were paved with sugared almonds and sugar trees bore ripe sugar lemons and apricots. After the fabulous creations were paraded through the streets for all to see, they were shared with the crowds. In 1675, on the eleventh day of the festivities surrounding the circumcision of the eldest son of Sultan Mehmed IV, one thousand trays of sweets were set on the ground for the crowds to eat. According to the Turkish historian Mary Işin, these celebrations were so spectacular that creating the sweetmeats was a multinational effort. In addition to hundreds of local confectioners, experts from Venice and the Greek island of Chios were hired to help create the decor.[12]

The elaborate displays and sugar sculptures could be rented or purchased, if one did not have the requisite help. During the eighteenth century, on the most fashionable dining tables, sugar sculptures were replaced by elegant porcelain displays made by new manufacturers such as Meissen, Sèvres and Wedgwood.

BANQUETING CONCEITS

Among the many conceits of the banquet, marzipan was one of the most versatile. The almond and sugar paste was shaped, moulded, modelled and coloured to make all sorts of fanciful figures, from hams and bacon to pears and oranges. Marzipan likely originated in sixth-century Persia, where sugar refining was sophisticated and almonds flourished. By the late Middle Ages, the delicious sweetmeat had spread to Sicily, Venice, Spain and Portugal and throughout Europe. Marzipan is not only an excellent modelling medium; it is delectable. As a result, marzipan figures were usually eaten soon after they were displayed, sometimes to the dismay of their creator. No less a talent than Leonardo da Vinci sculpted marzipan figures and then complained, 'I have observed with pain that my signor Ludovico and his court gobble up all the sculptures I give them, right to the last morsel,' he wrote, 'and now I am determined to find other means that do not taste as good, so that my works may survive.'[13]

Today, dazzling arrays of realistic-looking pears, watermelons, pomegranates, tomatoes and other fruits and vegetables made from marzipan are sold in shops throughout Europe and the United States. Some are filled with candied egg yolk or jam, some with chocolate, and some are dusted with confectioners' sugar. They are a prominent feature of dessert tables at both Christmas and Easter, when marzipan lambs join the assortment.

Whoever first had the happy idea of combining sugar and almonds to make the malleable and delicious sweet, cloistered nuns in Spain, Portugal, Italy and Sicily helped ensure its longevity. Throughout religious upheavals, wars and strife, the nuns made and sold their marzipan and other sweetmeats to support their convents. They sold them locally, and they also sent them off with missionaries and explorers and spread their sweetness throughout the world. A clever arrangement was created so that cloistered nuns could sell their marzipan and other sweets without coming into contact with buyers. Although rare today, the practice still exists in a few locations. At the seventeenth-century Convento de Corpus Cristi, at the Plaza de Conde de Miranda in Madrid, the sisters sell almond biscuits, *naranines* (orange sweets) and other pastries, rather than marzipan, but the experience is the same. Built into the wall of the convent's entryway, there is a turntable – rather like a miniature revolving door made of wood – that allows the transaction to take place without the visitors and nuns seeing each other. A list of pastries is posted on the wall next to the turntable. Visitors consult the list, make their choices, place the order and the money on the base of the turntable, and turn it around. In a few minutes, the turntable revolves again, this time with packages of the requested sweets.

Marzipan is one of the confectionery specialities in Toledo, Spain.

'Marchpane', often listed as a banquet conceit, sounds as if it were simply another way to spell marzipan. However, it is a separate, though related, entity. To make it, the cook or confectioner first made almond paste and rolled it out with a rolling pin, like pie pastry, and formed an edge around it 'as you do about a Tart', according to the anonymous author of the 1659 edition of *The Compleat Cook*. Then it was set on wafers and baked. The author titled his recipe 'To make a Marchpane: to Ice him, &c.' and wrote that after the first baking, one should 'Ice him with Rosewater and Sugar', and then spread on with a 'Wing-feather'. When it was done, the cook was to 'stick long Cumfets upright in him, so serve it'.[14] This recipe does not indicate how large the marchpane should be. A few years later, a recipe in Sir Kenelme Digby's book *The Closet of the Eminently Learned Sir Kenelme Digby Kt. Opened* (1671) specified that the marchpanes should be rolled out to about the size of one's hand and the thickness of a finger.[15]

Like many men of his era, Digby collected recipes from his friends. His were assembled posthumously and published by his assistant, George Hartman. A multi-talented man, Digby was a knight, a writer and a naval officer. Renowned in European scientific, philosophical and math-matical circles, he is considered the father of the modern wine bottle. During the 1630s, when he owned a glassworks, he manufactured wine bottles with a tapered neck, a collar and a punt – the indentation at the base of the bottle. Also a bibliophile, Digby is credited with preserving many valued manuscripts and books, which he donated to Oxford's Bodleian Library and the Bibliothèque nationale in Paris. In 1655 he donated forty books to the nascent Harvard College in Cambridge, Massachusetts.[16] He also was among the first to recommend bacon

The most elegant *anguillas*, or eels, are made from marzipan.

and eggs for breakfast, writing, 'Two poched [sic] eggs with a few fine dry-fryed Collops of pure Bacon, are not bad for breakfast, or to begin a meal.'[17]

Digby's recipe for marchpanes differed in some specifics from that of *The Compleat Cook*. He did not raise an edge around them. He baked them on papers and flipped them over during the baking process so that they would not scorch. He said that they should be dry on the outside but moist and tender inside. He iced his marchpanes with a mixture of egg whites, sugar and either orange-flower water or rosewater. When they were completed, he wrote, they should be 'pure, white, and smooth like silver between polished and matte, or like a looking-glass'.

Confectioners also used marchpanes as platforms for their elaborate sugar sculptures. In 1562 Queen Elizabeth was presented with a marchpane bearing a model of St Paul's Cathedral.[18] Those who found marchpanes too challenging to make could, if they had the means, purchase them ready-made from a confectioner. *Calissons*, the almond candies that the town of Aix-en-Provence is so famous for, are descendants of marchpanes.

FORK, KNIFE AND SPOON

On a cold winter's day, what could be better than tasting the sunny flavour of banqueting conceits like preserved orange peels or ginger in sugar syrup? Candied, sugar-strewn sweetmeats glistening in the candlelight of a banquet table looked dazzling and tasted wonderful. They turned fruits and berries into year-round pleasures rather than seasonal ones and had the added benefit of showing off the wealth of the host. Sugar, like honey, is an excellent preservative. Long before commercial bottling or refrigeration, when shipping involved long, perilous sea voyages, cooks knew that fruits kept safely if cooked in honey or sugar and could be enjoyed in any season. Preserved fruits were also appreciated because fresh fruits were considered dangerous, and sweetmeats were thought to be medicinal. 'Beware of green Sallets and raw fruits, for they will make your Lord sick,' advised William Rabisha in his book *The Whole Body of Cookery Dissected, Taught, and fully manifested Methodically, Artificially, and according to the best Tradition of the English, French, Italian, Dutch, &c.* (1673).[19]

Cookbooks of the sixteenth and seventeenth centuries include similar, if not identical, recipes for a variety of sweetmeats. In the 1611 edition of *The Closet for Ladies and Gentlewomen*, the anonymous author included a section on candying ginger, barberries, gooseberries, cherries, various roots and citrons, as well as violets, marigolds and 'all sorts of flowers, fruits, and spices'. Most of the recipes end with the phrase 'and keepe them all the yeare'. By then, most cooks were using sugar to preserve their fruits, but Digby's recipe titled 'To keep Quinces all the year good' was made with honey.[20]

Such sweetmeats were called suckets or succade and were differentiated as wet or dry. Wet suckets were fruits, peels and roots preserved and served in sugar syrup. They were part of the banquet course, and their stickiness gave rise to the use of the sucket fork. Dry suckets, also featured in the banquet, were fruits and other foods that were preserved in sugar syrup, drained, covered with sugar and dried in a warm oven.

In *The Queen's Royal Cookery*, author T. Hall directed the cook to strew the fruits with sugar three or four times while they were drying. He wrote that they should be sugared 'as you would do flour upon fish to fry them'. This is his recipe 'To candie barberries':

> First preserve them, then dip them quickly into warm Water to wash off the ropy Syrup, then strew them over with seared Sugar, and set them into an Oven or Stove three or four hours, always turning them, and casting more fine Sugar upon them, and never suffer them to be cold till they be dryed, and begin to look like Diamonds.[21]

American silver sucket forks, 17th century.

Many recipes attributed specific medical benefits to suckets. Candied eringo roots, a sea holly, were prized for their aphrodisiac qualities and popular in England and other European countries in the seventeenth and eighteenth centuries. Digby made suckets from lettuce stalks and from the stalks of mallows. He recommended candying the mallow stalks in spring when they were young and tender, cooking them in sugar syrup, and then taking them off the fire and letting them soak overnight. The next day, they had to be cooked again. He repeated the process 'six, or eight, or nine times . . . till they are sufficiently imbibed with the Syrup'. At that point, he wrote that they could be kept as a wet sucket in syrup or dried in a stove. Digby wrote that he liked them best dry, but soft and moist within. 'In Italy they eat much of them,' he wrote, 'for sharpness and heat of Urine.' He also said they were good for relieving the pain of gonorrhoea.[22]

Spoons have been scooping up soups and gruels since ancient times, and probably evolved from shells. Knives were weapons, and since hosts did not typically provide cutlery for their guests, diners used their own knives' sharp, pointed ends to spear morsels of food at the table. Forks, generally two-pronged, were serving tools. They were not considered necessary for eating. In fact, they were generally disdained. However, in the fifteenth century, Italian nobles and wealthy merchants began using personal sucket or sweetmeat forks. Smaller than our table forks, the delicate two-pronged sucket forks were useful for spearing sticky dry suckets. For wet suckets, special forks were designed with prongs on one end and a spoon bowl on the other. Diners picked up the fruit with the fork end and scooped up the syrup at the bottom of the dish with the spoon end.

Initially considered an effete affectation, forks met with considerable resistance. Some considered them irreligious. Not only did the prongs resemble the Devil's horns, but using a fork implied that food, which was a gift from God, was not good enough to be touched with one's hands.[23] However, forks gradually gained acceptance in European countries from Italy to France, Switzerland, Germany, the Netherlands,

England and, during the sixteenth and seventeenth centuries, the Scandinavian countries. By the end of the seventeenth century, silver sucket forks were being produced in Boston, Massachusetts. The forks were as decorative as they were practical. Most were made of silver, often with intricate designs, and some were inlaid or embellished with mother of pearl, amber, ivory or glass beads. Sweetmeat forks were used for nearly two centuries before the three-tined table fork came into general use in the early eighteenth century.

The word 'sucket' is now archaic, but we still enjoy candied ginger and add candied citrus peel to puddings and other sweet dishes. Fruits preserved in sugar syrup are a favourite sweet in Cyprus, Crete and many villages in Greece. Called spoon sweets, some are sold commercially, but the best are homemade. If you are fortunate enough to visit someone's home in the afternoon, the woman of the house will typically serve a bowl of glistening spoon sweets, along with a glass of cold water. The women make them with plums, cherries, orange rinds, figs, grapes, unripe green walnuts, quinces or even carrots. They are cooked in sugar syrup, put in sterilized glass jars and kept for months, to be ready whenever a guest arrives. Eaten with spoons rather than sucket forks, they are suckets by another name.

SERVICE À LA FRANÇAISE AND A DESSERT COURSE

The seventeenth century brought enormous change to the world of elite European dining. New books and theories concerning food and health appeared. Cookbooks were more available and often translated and disseminated across borders. Belief in humoral theory declined. Sugar lost its magical medicinal power, and some even associated it with the disease we know as diabetes. Savoury and sweet separated. Sugar no longer tempered savoury dishes, and rather than being consumed throughout the meal, it began its move to the end of the meal. Which is not to say that less sugar was consumed. When its cost declined as a result of New World plantations, slave labour and increased numbers of refineries, it moved down the social ladder. No longer restricted to the upper classes, sugar became available to nearly everyone. It was especially useful in sweetening the new (to Europeans) coffee, tea and chocolate drinks.

The service of meals changed as well. Gradually *service à la française* became the norm not only in France but throughout Europe. It continued to be the practice until the nineteenth century. Rather than covering the table with a profusion of dishes, as previously, dishes were placed according to a carefully laid-out symmetrical pattern. Along with recipes and menus, cookbooks commonly included diagrams of table layouts to ensure proper placement. There was a place for everything – and for a proper dinner, everything had to be in its place.

Typically three or four courses were served, although there were still as many as a dozen or more dishes for each. Recipes often suggested the appropriate place for a dish, whether for a corner or for a middle at supper or a centrepiece for a grand table. The first course consisted of a soup, served in an elaborate tureen and placed at the centre of the table. If two tureens were required, they would be set at either end, with a smaller platter of meat in the centre. Medium-sized platters of various foods would be placed at the four corners of the table, with smaller platters between them. Eight small dishes, the *hors d'oeuvres*, were arranged alongside the main dishes. The place settings for the diners were around the table's edge.

When the first course was finished, it was replaced by the second course, with a large roast placed at the centre. The roast could be meat or fish, and it need not have been actually roasted. It might have been prepared another way, but it was the large centrepiece of the course. It, too, would be surrounded by smaller offerings arranged according to the plan. The third course would feature the most impressive dessert in the centre, surrounded with smaller sweet dishes. A more elaborate dinner would present a variety of sweet *entremets* before the final dessert course.

EERSTE TAFEL.   PREMIERE TABLE.

TWEEDE TAFEL.   DEUXIÈME TABLE.

DERDE TAFEL.   TROISIEME TABLE.

VIERDE OF GROOTE TAFEL.   QUATRIEME OU GRANDE TABLE.

REPRESENTATION du DESSERT des QUATRE PRINCIPALES TABLES, au FESTIN, donné le 19 Janvier 1746 par Son Excellence Monsieur le BARON DE REISCHACH, Ministre Impérial à la Haye, à l'occasion de l'ELECTION et du COURONNEMENT de SA MAJESTÉ IMPERIALE.

Festivities in honour of the Emperor Francis I in 1747 warranted four principal tables with elaborate dessert courses for each one.

In the grandest establishments, the first courses would have
been prepared in the kitchen or *cuisine* by the *cuisinier*. The desserts
were the responsibility of the *office*, the smaller cooler kitchen where
the *officier* prepared jellies, marzipans, creams and other cold dishes,
and created sugarworks. By the eighteenth century, when chocolate,
ices and ice creams, and cakes became fashionable, they were made
there as well. This delegation of work was seen in cookbooks as well
as kitchens; those written by *cuisiniers* seldom included sweets. In
France, both the *cuisine* and the *office* were staffed by men. In England,
the large kitchens were usually staffed by men and, particularly after
the Restoration, often Frenchmen. However, women might be cooks

In this 17th-century Netherlands pastry shop, men do the baking and the female
proprietress tends to the sales.

in smaller households and in the English equivalent of the *office*, the cold kitchen, as well as the stillroom and the dairy.[24] Wealthy households in Italy employed French cooks or Italian cooks who had trained in France. In Naples and Sicily, they were called *monzus*, a corruption of the French *messieurs*. By the nineteenth century, French cooks were employed in court kitchens throughout Europe. Also spreading the French style and recipes were the many cookbooks published in French and translated into English, German, Swedish and other languages.

The word 'chef' was not used until the middle of the eighteenth century, when François Menon, one of the eighteenth century's most influential and prolific cookbook writers, referred to himself as a chef in his *Les Soupers de la cour*.[25] *Chef de cuisine* became the term used for the head of the kitchen; *Chef d'office* or *pâtissier*, for the head of the pastry kitchen.

The seventeenth-century changes in cuisine were presaged by Bartolomeo Scappi's *Opera* (1570) in Italy, Marx Rumpolt's *Ein New Kochbuch* (1581) in Germany and Hugh Platt's *Delights for Ladies* (1600) in England. But it was François Pierre La Varenne's *Le Cuisinier françois* (1651) that is credited with ushering in the new era in cuisine and the end of cookery's Middle Ages. His methods, organization and new recipes set the standard. The book was translated into English in 1653, and remained in print for more than 75 years. A second book, *Le Pâtissier françois*, published anonymously just two years afterwards, was also attributed to La Varenne, although there is doubt about the identity of its author. In any event, it brought the same codified approach to the works of the office. The author offered specifics on weights, measurements and temperatures, and recipes for different pastry doughs and pastry creams. *Le Pâtissier françois* provided recipes for macaroons, sweet pies and tarts, sponge cake and puff pastry. It was the first work to mention the small ovens called *petit fours*, which, in the nineteenth century, gave their name to France's famed frosted miniature cakes.[26]

The ability to work with sugar was critical to the art of the pastry chef, and as a result many confectionery cookbooks and professional manuals began with an explanation of the various stages of sugar boiling. François Massialot, one of the few cooks who was equally proficient in both the kitchen and the pastry kitchen, began his book *Nouvelle instruction pour les confitures, les liqueurs, et les fruits* (1692) with a chapter on selecting, clarifying and cooking with sugar. He described six sugar syrup stages: *lissé* or thread; *perlé*, pearl; *soufflé*, blow; *plume*, feather; *cassé*, crack; and *caramel*. These distinctions are more impressive when one realizes that cooks did not yet have thermometers. They were judging the stages by touch, smell and appearance. Like other confectioners of his time, Massialot tested some of the stages by dipping his index finger into the hot syrup, touching his finger to his thumb and drawing the digits apart. He determined the stage by the thickness of the thread thus created and the time it took to break.

Massialot's books were quickly translated into English and were influential among the aristocratic English Whigs who relished fashionable French style. *Le Cuisinier roïal et bourgeois* was translated into English as *The Court and Country Cook* in 1702. It was divided into two sections. In the first section, Massialot listed menu items for a dinner in the month of January, but wrote of the third course, 'This is to consist of Fruits and Confits, of which we shall say nothing in this place; that being the particular Business of another Officer and not of the Cook.'[27]

The section titled *New Instructions for Confectioners* began with the stages of cooking sugar and included many recipes for preserving fruits in sugar syrups, and making marmalades, jellies, comfits and marchpanes. But among these typical recipes were also more contemporary ones. There were recipes for meringues filled with preserved fruit, put together to make 'twins'. Massialot had recipes for puff pastry, macaroons, which he explained were 'a particular Confection of sweet Almonds, Sugar, and the White of an Egg', and wafers rolled into cone shapes on a wooden implement 'made for that purpose'.

In a section on arranging banquets, Massialot suggested filling small, decorated baskets with sweetmeats for guests to take home

This 18th-century
Spanish dessert table
is set for thirty.

to their families and friends, and recommended that the guests
themselves eat only the liquid sweetmeats such as marmalades or the
fresh fruits. Another section, which is reassuring to anyone who has
had a dessert go awry, was titled, 'Of the Accidents that may happen
to Sweet-Meats, and of proper Means for the remedying of them'.[28]

CHANGE IS NOT EASY

Change came slowly to the dessert course. Bartolomeo Stefani, who
was the principal cook at the Gonzaga court in Mantua and the author
of *L'arte di ben cucinare, et instruire* (The Art of Cooking Well, with
Instructions), published in 1662, still used such flavourings as musk,
ambergris and rosewater, and served comfits, candied pumpkin, candied citron and conserves of various fruits and flowers for his desserts.[29]

The influential Patrick Lamb was court cook for Charles II, James
II, King William and Queen Mary, and Queen Anne. His book *Royal
Cookery; or, The Compleat Court-cook* (1710) clung to the past. Many of
the table settings illustrated in the book combined sweet and savoury
within a single course. A plan for a cold wedding supper showed a

large pyramid of sweetmeats in the place of honour at the centre of the table. It was flanked by small dishes of jellies. However, they were encircled by plates of chicken, lamb and other savoury dishes as well as cheeses, cakes and custards.

A towering pyramid of sweetmeats was often featured as a centrepiece. To stabilize the precarious arrangements, a dish might be inserted between every few layers. The dishes were called *pourcelaines*, although they might be made from silver, pewter or tin as well as porcelain. Madame de Sévigné, whose letters are filled with information and gossip about seventeenth-century French society, described a dinner at which disaster struck one of the lofty pyramids. She wrote that it was made with twenty *pourcelaines*, and when it tipped over, the noise was so deafening that it drowned out the music.[30]

The trade card of this well-stocked London shop advertises such fashionable 18th-century goods as sugar, chocolate, coffee and tea.

Service à la française spread throughout Europe, but some English cooks resented the prevalence of French style. In the prefaces to their books, English cooks complained about the extravagance of French food, wrote about the superiority of English meats and produce, and claimed to eschew foreign dishes, although they always included recipes for them in their books. English cooks were understandably dismayed at the upper-class tendency to hire French cooks and pay them more generously than English ones.

Charles Carter, author of the cookbook *The Compleat City and Country Cook; or, Accomplish'd Housewife* (1732), noted that he had cooked for dukes and earls and worked in Flanders, Berlin, Spain and Portugal, as well as England. He was displeased by the French influence and wrote,

> Some of our Nobility and Gentry have been too much attach'd
> to French Customs and French Cookery, so that they have not
> thought themselves capable of being well serv'd, unless they sent
> for a Cook from a Foreign Country, who, indeed by the Poverty
> of his Country (compar'd with our own) and the flippant Humour
> of its Inhabitants, whose Gousts [tastes] are continually changing,
> is constrain'd to rack his Invention to disguise Nature and lose it
> in Art, rather to puzzle than please the Palate.[31]

Most of Carter's meal plans are for two-course dinners with a second course featuring a sweet pie or tart as the centrepiece, and savoury dishes all around it. But for a special occasion he had a separate dessert course, which he called 'Desart'. Its centrepiece was a pyramid of sweetmeats, surrounded by lemon and pistachio creams, biscuits, peaches, nectarines, apricots, jellies and the creams called 'syllabubs'.

Some Englishmen did praise French food. Arthur Young, who wrote about agriculture, travelled in France during the Revolutionary era. Although he feared the coming Revolution, he praised the French art of living. He wrote,

> Of their cookery, there is but one opinion; for every man in
> Europe, that can afford a great table, either keeps a French cook,
> or one instructed in the same manner . . . they dress an hundred
> dishes in an hundred different ways, and most of them excellent
> . . . A regular dessert with us is expected, at a considerable table
> only, or at a moderate one when a formal entertainment is given;
> in France it is as essential to the smallest dinner as to the largest;
> if it consists only of a bunch of dried grapes, or an apple, it will
> be as regularly served as the soup.[32]

The French confectioner Joseph Gilliers produced detailed plans of his desserts and table settings in his 1768 book, *Le Cannameliste français*.

Echelle de   1 2 3 4 5 6 7 8 9 10 11 12 13 14 15 16 17 18 19 20 21 22 23 24 25 26 Pieds

Fig. 1.

PASTRY AS ARCHITECTURE

The design of table decor largely followed the style of the art of its era. The baroque sweetmeat pyramids that pastry chefs designed in the seventeenth century were followed by neoclassical statuary in the eighteenth. During the Romantic era, tables featured crumbling classical ruins.[33] Such artistic sugarwork was the mark of an accomplished pastry chef, and the master was Marie-Antoine Carême, generally known as Antonin Carême. The first celebrity chef, Carême personified French culinary excellence and elegance. Both a *chef de cuisine* and a pastry chef, his elaborate sugar sculptures, or *pièces montées*, were renowned. He created artistic, often architectural, centrepieces that graced the grandest tables wherever he worked, from France to England to Russia.

Carême had an unlikely career. Abandoned to the streets of Paris by his parents during the violent years of the French Revolution when he was not yet in his teens, he was fortunate to have survived. But he was resourceful. He found kitchen work, and then was taken on as an apprentice by a pastry maker. He not only learned his craft, but educated himself in architecture by studying prints in the Bibliothèque nationale, eventually recreating the designs in table-top structures made from sugar, pastry, confectioners' paste and meringue. He is thought to have been the first to pipe meringue using a pastry bag. (Previously it was shaped with a spoon.) Carême considered cuisine a branch of architecture and enjoyed being called the Palladio of French cuisine. For a dinner celebrating a christening in Vienna in 1821, he made a Roman villa, a Venetian fountain, an Irish pavilion on a bridge and a Persian pavilion on a rocky outcrop – all in addition to a menu of 32 different dishes, from soups to jellies. He instituted the codification of French sauces and popularized such still-familiar desserts as soufflés, Bavarian cream, Nesselrode pudding and many more.[34]

During the course of his career, Carême worked for Napoleon and his foreign minister, Charles Maurice de Talleyrand, the Russian

Tsar Alexander I, England's Prince Regent and the Rothschilds in Paris. His influence spread as he shared his system of kitchen organization, recipes and creations through his many publications. Carême wrote and illustrated books, including *Le Pâtissier royal parisien* (1815), *Le Pâtissier pittoresque* (1816), *Le Maître d'hôtel français* (1822), *Le Cuisinier parisien* (1828) and *L'Art de la cuisine française au XIXe siècle*, which was completed after his death in 1833, when he was not quite fifty years old.

SERVICE À LA RUSSE

During the nineteenth century, the flaws in *service à la française* were becoming apparent. It was beginning to feel excessive in an era that was becoming less formal. Despite the artistry of the arrangement, there was still too much food on the table at one time. As a result, dishes grew cold before they could be enjoyed. The contemporary style in Russia was sequential service, with dishes plated and served as they are today in most restaurants. Fewer dishes were served, and it therefore

Dinner for eight in 1874, with the table set *à la russe* style.

allowed the food to be served at the proper temperature. *Service à la russe* valued dining over display. The style spread from Russia to France, Germany, Britain and eventually the U.S. As a result of his time in Russia, Carême was familiar with the disadvantages of the French style and the advantages of the Russian style. But he still preferred *service à la française* because it allowed him to flaunt his artistry.

Despite Carême's resistance, during the second half of the nineteenth century, after the French Revolution, the simpler and more practical *service à la russe* gradually took over. The fantastic displays of chefs like Carême largely disappeared, and fresh flowers took the place of sugar temples and *pourcelaines* on dining tables. Sometimes an elaborate dessert would be displayed on the dining table or on a side table throughout the meal to add visual appeal, but the era of towering, and sometimes crashing, sweet structures was coming to an end.

IN MANY COUNTRIES there might be two sweet courses at the end of a meal. In France, *entremets* consisting of dishes such as Bavarian creams would be followed by another dessert consisting of cakes or fruits. In England, often the penultimate course of a meal would be a pie or tart, and then the tablecloth would be removed and the second sweet course of fruits, nuts and sweetmeats would be served. The anonymous author of *The Whole Duty of a Woman; or, An Infallible Guide to the Fair Sex*, published in 1737, wrote,

> When the Desert is to come on, Care must be taken to see the Table well cleared, and the upper Table-Cloth taken off, with the Leather which lay between that and the under one. Dry'd Sweetmeats, Sweetmeats in Glasses and Fruits, are placed in Pyramids, or otherwise, like the great Dishes of Meat.[35]

Years later, some writers would suggest that removing the tablecloth to serve sweetmeats was a way to show off expensive mahogany tables. In the mid-nineteenth century, the famed chef and reformer

Alexis Soyer published *The Modern Housewife or Ménagère*. In addition to nearly one thousand recipes, the book included a series of fictional letters between Mrs B. and Mrs L. concerning household management and proper entertaining. In one, Mrs B. says that when they entertain friends at dinner, they have the tablecloth removed for the dessert service. She explains that Mr B. 'likes to see the mahogany, for when he asks a City friend to come and put his feet under his mahogany, it looks rather foolish if he never sees it'.[36]

Concluding dinner with a separate and distinct dessert course became the norm in most of Europe and England, but it was not the practice everywhere. In Turkey, dinners included sweets amid the plethora of other dishes, just as they had in earlier times in other countries. During the late nineteenth century, however, Europeans were so accustomed to the separation of sweets and savouries that they were nonplussed when they were served sweet dishes in the middle of dinner.

TURKISH DELIGHTS

Lady Agnes Ramsay accompanied her husband, a prominent English archaeologist, to Turkey in the nineteenth century and wrote about her travels in *Every-day Life in Turkey*. Writing primarily about her experiences in the villages where she and her husband often spent their nights in tents or less-than-salubrious inns, she said she wanted to correct the opinion held by many Europeans that Turks were a vicious lot. To the contrary, she found them to be 'simple, peaceable, hospitable, and friendly'. She was invited into their homes and even visited a harem. Lady Ramsay liked nearly all the food, from modest meals of yoghurt, bread, tomatoes and olives to elaborate multi-course dinners. She was especially complimentary about Turkish sweets. But, at one dinner, she was chagrined to discover that the meal was not concluded after the cream-filled baklava was served. In fact, it had only just begun.

She did not care for the rice dish served as the first course, but she enjoyed the next, a roasted calf. She called it the 'fatted calf'. Then came what she thought was the dessert, the final course – 'the cream tart of the *Arabian Nights*'. She wrote,

> It was about eighteen inches in diameter and the colour
> of its crust was a gleaming golden brown. I will not attempt
> to describe the exquisite lightness of the flaky pastry or the
> delicate fragrance of the rich cream which filled it! To
> properly appreciate cream tart one must eat it. A dream
> of my childhood had been realised.

Lady Ramsay was ready to rise from the table. But to her surprise, there was more to come. Next were 'dolmadhés . . . a delicious dish when one is hungry; but by this time I was the reverse'. They were followed by cherries cooked in honey, a roasted kid stuffed with pistachios, and more sweets, fowls, vegetables and fruits. Meats and

Baklava, one of the Turkish pastries Lady Ramsay loved.

Today, at the Serraikon bakery in Kilkis, Greece, women stretch the filo dough for flaky pastries like those enjoyed by Lady Agnes Ramsay by hand; they swirl the dough in the air until it's thin enough to read through.

sweets alternated in 'hideous succession . . . Daylight died out, lamps were lit, and still the dreadful feast went on'. Finally a pilaf was served, and she noted with relief, though incorrectly, that '*pilaf* is always the last dish at a Turkish dinner.'[37]

Dessert did not always know its place.[38]

THREE

DELIGHTS FROM THE DAIRY

LIKE ROSES, CREAMS BY any other name smell and taste as sweet. Crème anglaise, *crema catalana*, leache, snow, syllabub, custard, flan, flawn, fool, milk pudding, Bavarian cream, clotted cream, *crème Chantilly*, *lattemiele*, *schlagober*, panna cotta, *pudim flan*, *pudim veludo*, crème brûlée – the list goes on. From England to Argentina, from Barcelona to Bruges, under countless names, creams please the pampered, satisfy the hungry and sooth the sick.

As nearly universally loved as creamy dishes are, however, their prominence has waxed and waned over time. During some periods, they were seen as food for simple folk. At others, they were largely for elites. In England, during the seventeenth and eighteenth centuries, as a result of the Enclosure laws, land previously open to common grazing by village livestock was closed off, and its use was limited to well-off landowners. Dairy products became too expensive for the rural poor, whose children often developed rickets as a result. The gentry not only had dairy products, but revelled in them. Hitherto considered humble foods, creamy dishes from milk puddings to syllabubs became fashionable among the upper classes.

Everything about dairying was in vogue. Milkmaids were idealized and associated with purity and femininity. They were depicted in storybooks and prints suitable for framing, which well-off citizens collected. Apple-cheeked milkmaids were painted wearing picturesque outfits, often with delicate lace-trimmed petticoats peeking out from

'The merry Milk Maid' is one of the street traders depicted in the 1688 *Cries of London*.

their skirts. Even if milkmaids could have afforded such clothing, it was hardly practical for milking cows or carrying pails of milk to market.

The fashion for seemingly simple pastimes led to the construction of pleasure dairies on grand estates in England, France, Russia and other countries. Ladies had dairies built where they could enjoy the pastoral life, entertain friends, sip milk warm from a cow, and possibly churn a bit of butter or whip some cream. Known in France as *laiteries d'agrément*, pleasure dairies were separate from working dairies, *laiteries de préparation*, to keep unpleasantness like the odour of cows

The creamery at the royal dairy at Frogmore, near Windsor Castle.

away. Catherine de' Medici's mid-sixteenth-century pleasure dairy at Fontainebleau was one of the earliest. Marie-Antoinette famously played milkmaid at Versailles, and there were pleasure dairies at Chantilly, Raincy and other locations in France.[1] In 1783 Maria Feodorovna, Grand Duchess of Russia, had one built at her palace near St Petersburg.[2] On English estates, pleasure dairies, also known as ornamental dairies, had a slightly less frivolous image. They were intended to demonstrate the landowners' engagement with the land, to show that they were responsible custodians of their properties and that they were committed to rural values.

Pleasure dairies everywhere were primarily a feminine realm. They gave the lady of the household a place to be as industrious or entertaining as she chose. They were especially popular during the eighteenth century (though they were built earlier as well), reflecting the Romantic vogue for a return to nature and a simpler way of life, a style that was influenced by the writings of philosopher Jean-Jacques Rousseau. However, these were not modest structures. Designed by the best-known architects of the day, they recreated Greek temples, Gothic castles and Swiss chalets. Built of marble or stone, with walls lined with Wedgwood tiles or decorated with bucolic paintings, they featured elegant fountains and marble counters. Queen Mary II began the trend in the late seventeenth century in England by having an ornamental dairy decorated with blue-and-white Delft tiles from King William's native Holland built at Hampton Court. Others followed her lead. Countess Spencer's dairy at Althorp, Northamptonshire, was built in 1786 in Romantic rustic style.[3] A few years later, the Duke of Bedford had an elaborate Chinese-style dairy built at Woburn Abbey, Bedfordshire. In 1858 Prince Albert had a Victorian Gothic-style dairy built at the Home Farm at Frogmore, complete with majolica-tiled walls and stained-glass windows.

The concept of entertaining in the dairy moved down the social scale as well. Isabella Beeton, the English author of the famed nineteenth-century tome *The Book of Household Management*, wrote for the bourgeois household, not for royalty. However, in the book, which was popularly referred to simply as 'Mrs Beeton', she called the dairy the 'temple in which the dairy-maid presides', and wrote that because guests as well as the mistress of the house sometimes visited the dairy, it should be not only scrupulously clean but 'ornamental and picturesque'.[4]

Dairies were fashionable spaces where ladies could entertain their neighbours, display their fine china and make, or serve, syllabubs and flummeries for their friends. At the very least, they were places to enjoy the creamy desserts they loved.

CRÈMES DE LA CRÈME

Creams abound in cookbooks. When Mrs Mary Eales published the first recipe in English for ice cream in 1718, her instructions began 'Take Tin Ice-Pots, fill them with any Sort of Cream you like, either plain or sweeten'd, or Fruit in it . . .', and went on to explain the freezing process. She did not need to be more specific, because preceding the ice-cream recipe were recipes for more than a dozen different creams, from almond to pistachio to 'all sorts of Fruit-Cream'. Any one of them could be used as a base for ice cream. Also among her creams was a recipe for 'Trout-Cream'. Happily, it did not call for fish. It was flavoured with orange-flower water, moulded into the shape of a fish and served surrounded by whipped cream. Cooks have always enjoyed disguising foods as things they are not – a habit that would reach its peak when ice cream became more commonplace.[5]

François Massialot's *The Court and Country Cook*, published in 1702, included nearly a dozen creams. He introduced them by writing, 'There are several sorts of Creams; particularly of Almonds and Pistachoes, burnt Cream, crackling Cream, fried Cream, Cream after the Italian Mode and some others.' He made a chocolate cream and a flour-thickened pastry cream for use in pies and tarts. On fast days, when dairy milk was prohibited, he first pounded and strained almonds to make almond milk and then proceeded to make his creams. His burnt cream is made like today's crème brûlée, except for the tool used to caramelize the topping. He instructed the cook to 'take a Fire-shovel heated red-hot, and at the same time, burn the Cream with it, to give it a fine Gold-colour'.[6]

His recipe for 'Chocolate-cream' would be called chocolate pudding today in the u.s. The word 'walm' means a bubble or boil, despite the fact that such a mixture should not boil as that tends to scramble the egg. Perhaps Massialot meant simmer rather than boil, or it could be that he directed readers to strain the mixture because it did scramble.

> Take a Quart of Milk with a quarter of a Pound of Sugar, and boil them together for a quarter of an Hour; Then put one beaten Yolk of an Egg into the Cream, and let it have three or four Walms; Take it off from the Fire, and mix it with some Chocolate, til the Cream has assum'd its colour. Afterwards you may give it three or four Walms more upon the Fire, and, having strain'd it thro' a Sieve, dress it at pleasure.[7]

An American cookbook from 1913 titled *The Oriental Cook Book: Wholesome, Dainty and Economical Dishes of the Orient, especially adapted to American Tastes and Methods of Preparation*, by Ardashes H. Keoleian, included a recipe called 'Paklava with Cream', which is like the cream-filled baklava Lady Ramsay delighted in and described in *Everyday Life in Turkey*.[8] A Portuguese American cookbook, published in 1966, added a glass of port to its basic custard recipe.[9] The variations are endless.

DRINKING CREAMS AND EATING CREAMS

The warm, creamy alcoholic drinks called 'possets' date back to at least the sixteenth century. They were often served as a nightcap or even sipped in bed to help lull one to sleep. Lady Macbeth served toxic possets to Duncan's guards to make them fall into a deep sleep while Macbeth murdered their king. Generally, possets were more benign.

Hot posset drinks were originally made with milk cooked with ale, sack, claret or orange juice, and sugar. Ordinary folk turned the drinks into possets to be eaten by adding breadcrumbs to the mixture. The gentry had theirs made with cream, sack or brandy, eggs, grated biscuits or beaten almonds.[10] Some cooks spiced theirs up with ginger, nutmeg or cinnamon. Elizabeth Raffald, author of *The Experienced English Housekeeper*, flavoured her almond posset with rosewater and served it in a china bowl. She wrote, 'When you send it to table put in three macaroons to swim on the top.'[11]

A well-made posset separated into three layers: a frothy cream called the 'grace' floated on top, a smooth custard occupied the middle tier and warm ale or spirits lay below. Posset cups with spouts were created to allow one to scoop up the frothy top and the creamy centre with a spoon, and sip the liquid from the spout, which was set into the lower portion of the cup. The most elegant posset pots were made of china or silver in sets with covers and basins and made splendid presents.

Syllabubs, kissing cousin to possets, were desserts made by pouring milk or cream into sweetened hard cider, wine, sour orange juice or another acidic liquid to make the cream curdle. The main difference between possets and syllabubs is that possets were cooked and served warm, and syllabubs were (almost always) uncooked and served cool or cold. Both are related to the creamy, spirited drink we call eggnog. Syllabub was also spelled *sillabub, sullabub, sullybub, sillie bube* and *sillybob*. French cooks used such terms as *syllabub solide* and *syllabub sous la vache*.[12] Many recipes directed the cook to pour the cider into a punch bowl, sweeten it and then carry it out to a cow so the milk could be squirted directly from the cow to the container. The fresh warm milk gushing into the cider would create a froth. Then the mixture was to be left undisturbed for an hour or two, and the froth would turn into curds above, whey below. Sometimes fresh cream would be poured over it just before serving.

The English food historian Ivan Day enlisted a cow and made syllabub in just this way not long ago. His conclusion was that it was more problematic than the writers of early recipes implied, though he did make it work. As a result of his experience, Day suggested that recipe writers might have been merely copying previous recipes rather than employing a cow and attempting to make the syllabub themselves.[13]

Possibly because it was difficult or perhaps because there was no cow at hand, some recipes recommended pouring the milk or cream into the cider or wine from a height to make it froth, rather than squirting it from the cow into the liquor. Others employed an implement called

This English earthenware posset cup has a lid to keep the contents warm.

the wooden cow, a kind of syringe that forced the milk into the liquor with enough pressure to make the mixture froth.

Whipped syllabub, the version that became a highlight of eighteenth-century dessert tables, was made by whisking the cream and the wine mixture together until a layer of bubbles rose to the top. That layer was skimmed off and set on a sieve to drain. The process was repeated until all was used. The foam could drain for hours or even a day, until it was thoroughly dried and ready to be served. Mrs Raffald served hers by half filling glasses with wine, some red and some white, and then topping each glass with a cloud of whipped syllabub, for a very pretty arrangement. Like possets, syllabubs were often served in spouted glasses so that the liquid could be sipped and the whipped syllabub on top eaten with a spoon.

Another version, called everlasting syllabub, was made by using less wine, along with thick cream, sugar and lemon, and simply whisking the ingredients together until the mixture held its shape. It did not require skimming and draining. These syllabubs did not separate and lasted for days, if not forever. They also became the topping for trifles. Mrs Hannah Glasse included a recipe for 'Syllabub from the Cow', as well as recipes for 'Whipt', 'Everlasting' and 'Solid' syllabubs, in *The Art of Cookery Made Plain and Easy*.

TO MAKE SOLID SYLLABUBS

To a quart of rich cream put a pint of white-wine, the juice
of two lemons, the rind of one grated, sweeten it to your taste;
mill it with a chocolate mill till it is all of a thickness; then put
it in glasses, or a bowl, and set it in a cool place till next day.[14]

In their day, which lasted from the sixteenth through the nineteenth century, syllabubs were such a well-known dish that authors used the name metaphorically. A writer for a spring edition of the 1889 *London Daily News* could describe the season's new bonnets as 'mere syllabubs of frothed-up lace', and know that readers would understand

Back in popularity, today's syllabubs are still light and frothy desserts.

the bonnets were insubstantial and frilly. A character in Charlotte Brontë's *Shirley*, published in 1849, could ask, 'When did I whip up syllabub sonnets, or string stanzas fragile as fragments of glass?' and know she would be understood.[15] Everyone knew what light, frothy syllabubs were, because recipes and references were everywhere. In one version of a well-known nursery rhyme, the Queen of Hearts did not make tarts, the Queen of Clubs made syllabubs.

JELLIED MILK PUDDINGS

Many of the creams of the past have disappeared from today's dessert tables; others have remained popular or returned to popularity, sometimes with a different name. Still others have been transformed into quite different dishes. One of the earliest, called leach, dates back to the fourteenth century. The word is derived from the Anglo-Norman word for slices, so a leach (also spelled as *leache, leche, leech, lechemeat*) was a jelled, sliceable dish that might be made with meats, eggs or fruits. By Tudor times, leaches had become a jellied milk pudding usually made with almond milk. Dairy milk or cream came to be used by the early seventeenth century after the Reformation relaxed the rules having to do with fasting and abstaining from cow's milk. Leaches were jellied using calves' foot stock, isinglass (made from the air bladders of certain fish) or hartshorn (made from the antlers of harts or stags). They were sweetened with sugar, made rich with cream or milk and flavoured with rosewater and, often, almonds.

Whether lavished with gold leaf, left white or coloured red, leaches were a favourite dish for the banquet. During the Restoration era, Robert May flavoured one of his with rosewater, musk, mace and mace oil. When it was set, he cut it into slices like 'chequerwork' and said that was the best way to make it.

Mrs Raffald made a similar dish, but in 1769 when her book was published, the name had changed to flummery. Flummery had begun as a kind of jellied oatmeal, usually served with milk or cream, then evolved into a more sophisticated jellied pudding made without oatmeal, and merged with leach. Mrs Raffald made her basic flummery with a combination of sweet and bitter almonds and flavoured it with rosewater. Her flummeries were elegant, and her instructions were detailed. Rather than serving them in slices, she moulded them into various shapes. She instructed her reader to be sure to wet the moulds in cold water before pouring in the mixture so that it would turn out without the need to dip the moulds in warm water. That 'takes off the figures of the mould and makes the flummery look dull,' she wrote.[16]

Mrs Raffald coloured some of her flummeries pink with cochineal, yellow with saffron and green with spinach. She made decorative, even whimsical, flummeries. To create a pond of flummery fish swimming in a sea of clear jelly, she first moulded flummery into the shapes of four large fish and six small ones. She poured clear calves' foot jelly into a large bowl and, when it had set, she arranged two of the small fish on the jelly, right side down, and covered them with another layer of clear jelly. Then she arranged the other four small fish 'across one another, that when you turn the bowl upside down the heads and tails may be seen'. She added more jelly to set them in place, then placed the four large fish on top and filled the bowl with more clear jelly. The next day, she turned it upside down onto a serving platter. The effect must have been stunning.

Raffald titled another flummery recipe 'To make a Hen's Nest'.[17] To make it, she first made flummery, then poured it into small eggshells. Next, she filled a basin with clear calf's foot jelly. She candied lemon peel and shaped it into nests, which she set on the cooled and set jelly. When the flummery eggs were ready, she peeled off the shells and arranged them on the lemon nests. More than two centuries later and thousands of miles away, Holly Arnold Kinney, owner of the famed Fort restaurant in Colorado, recalled the storied Easter dessert that has been a tradition in her family for generations. Her grandmother, Katharine, made it. Her father, Sam Arnold, founder of the restaurant, and his sister Dr Mary Arnold made it. And now Kinney herself makes it every year. They call it Bird's Nest Pudding and describe the pudding as 'blancmange', but it is clearly a descendant of Mrs Raffald's flummery hen's nest. In her book, *Shinin' Times at The Fort*, Kinney wrote,

> This recipe is one I remember from my childhood and to this
> day I make it every Easter . . . As with so many of the dishes
> I love, I learned this one from my father, Sam'l. Here is what

An artist's depiction of Sam Arnold, young Holly and grandmother Katharine anticipating their Easter Bird's Nest Pudding.

he said about the pudding. 'Easter wasn't Easter at our house when I was a child without Bird's Nest Pudding. I have no idea where my mother learned the dish. It probably came from her mother's English Quaker ancestors, the Fox family.'

In the book, Kinney described saving eggshells for weeks before Easter Sunday and setting them aside to dry, and then making the blancmange, dividing it into batches and flavouring and colouring each one differently. Next she poured the blancmange into the eggshells to set and half filled a cut-glass serving bowl with a wine gelatine. Like Mrs Raffald, she candied fruit peel for the nests, although Kinney used orange and grapefruit peel rather than lemon peel. Finally, when all the components were ready, she arranged the nests on the gelatine and set the blancmange eggs carefully in their nests. The final dish was as festive on the twenty-first-century American table as it had been on the eighteenth-century English one.[18]

One of the most popular Danish puddings is called *rødgrød med
fløde*, which is translated as 'red fruit pudding with cream'. It is usually made with red berries and, unlike most flummeries, not with cream or milk, although it is generally topped with cream. Nevertheless, the recipe below for a variation using rhubarb – handed down the generations from a Danish grandmother to her American descendants – was always called 'Rhubarb flummery (A version of *rødgrød med fløde*)'. No one knows why. Perhaps she thought flummery was easier for Americans to pronounce, or possibly her neighbours in Maine used the word flummery. Holly Korda, a Maine resident of Danish heritage, contributed the recipe, which she inherited from her aunt Marion Korda, who inherited it from her grandmother, Amelia Thorsager Møller.

RHUBARB FLUMMERY (A VERSION OF *RØDGRØD MED FLØDE*)
4 cups (600 g) rhubarb in one-inch (2-cm) pieces
¾ cup (150 g) sugar
grated rind of one orange or lemon

Boysenberries give this flummery a lovely lavender tint and a hint of tartness.

½ cup (120 ml) water
3 tablespoons cornflour (cornstarch)

Combine rhubarb, sugar, orange rind and water in a saucepan.
Bring slowly to a boil, cover, and simmer for two to three minutes
or until rhubarb is soft but still holds its shape. Do not overcook.

Blend cornstarch with a small amount of cold water. Stir gently
into the rhubarb mixture. Bring to a boil and cook, stirring gently
until clear and thickened.

Pour into a serving dish and sprinkle with sugar. Serve slightly
warm with cream.

Serves 4 to 6

Flummery has disappeared from most cookbooks and dessert
tables, and the word is not much used today. But once, like syllabub,
it was a common enough word to be used outside the kitchen to mean
something slight and insubstantial – empty praise, humbug or useless

ornaments. Mark Twain, describing the decor of the bridal chamber
aboard a steamboat, wrote that its 'pretentious flummery was necessarily
overawing to the intellect of that hosannahing citizen'.[19]

A Colourful White Dish

A close relation of flummery, blancmange also dates back to the Middle
Ages and has undergone many changes over time. A truly international
dish, versions of blancmange were eaten in Italy, France, Spain,
Germany, Turkey and England, and eventually America. The great
Renaissance Italian guide to cooking, dining, foods and health,
Platina's *De honesta voluptate et valetudine* (On Right Pleasure and
Good Health), featured a *biancomangiare* recipe. The name, whether
blancmange, *biancomangiare* or *manjar blanco*, means 'white dish'.
But it was not always white. French cookbooks had instructions for
blanc manger parti, or parted, into different colours including red,
gold, blue and silver. Some nineteenth-century cookbooks have recipes
for chocolate blancmange, the ultimate oxymoron.

Originally the white dish was made with almond milk and
pounded capon flesh, cooked until thick, sweetened with sugar and
often perfumed with rosewater. It was served decorated with pomegranate seeds. Later recipes call for shredded chicken, or fish on fast
days when meat was prohibited, rice or hartshorn to thicken it, sugar
and almonds. In Turkey, a dish close to the original survives. Called
tavuk göğsü, chicken breast pudding, it is made with shredded chicken,
rice, milk and sugar and flavoured with cinnamon. It is served as a
dessert. In the Philippines, blancmange is made with water buffalo
milk, thickened with cornflour and sprinkled with toasted coconut.
It is informally called *tibok-tibok*, because when it is shaken, it quivers
as if it has a heartbeat.[20]

In most countries, the meat or fish disappeared from the dish
by the seventeenth century. La Varenne made it with chicken stock
rather than chicken meat. François Massialot introduced a version

of blancmange to England which was made without chicken or fish. He had two recipes for blancmange in *The Court and Country Cook*; although the first called for a hen, the pudding was strained to make it smooth. The second was made without fish or fowl. It used hartshorn shavings, pounded almonds, milk, cream and orange-flower water. It was becoming the creamy moulded blancmange of modern times. Various ingredients have been used to make blancmange gel so that it could be moulded and turned out onto a serving platter – isinglass, calves' feet, hartshorn, seaweed and, during the nineteenth century, arrowroot, cornflour and granulated gelatine. As they did with flummery, cooks moulded blancmange into many fanciful shapes and served it creatively. In the 1796 edition of *The Art of Cookery Made Plain and Easy*, author Hannah Glasse moulded blancmange into the shapes of a half-moon and stars and set them on a base of clear jelly.

The pristine elegance of unadorned blancmange.

She called the recipe 'Moon-shine'. Glasse's basic blancmange is a sweet cream, jellied with isinglass and flavoured with both rosewater and orange-flower water. She wrote, 'It makes a fine side-dish. You may eat it with cream, wine, or what you please. Lay round it baked pears. It both looks very pretty, and eats fine.'[21]

Blancmange became popular in America as well. In the Civil War-era novel *Little Women*, author Louisa May Alcott wrote that the March family served their blancmange 'surrounded by a garland of green leaves, and the scarlet flowers of Amy's pet geranium'.[22] Abigail Alcott, the mother of Louisa May, clipped a recipe for arrowroot blancmange from an unidentified newspaper and included it in the collection she called 'Receipts and simple recipes'. Maria Parloa, a highly regarded nineteenth-century American cook, cookbook author, home economist and teacher, wrote several influential cookbooks, as well as magazine columns and promotional pamphlets. She used Irish moss (a type of seaweed) to gel her blancmange in this recipe from *Miss Parloa's Young Housekeeper*:

MOSS BLANCMANGE

1 gill of Irish moss.	1 saltspoonful of salt.
1 quart of milk.	1 teaspoonful of vanilla extract.
2 tablespoonfuls of sugar.	

Measure the moss loosely. Wash it and pick out all the pebbles and seaweed. Continue washing it until every particle of sand is removed. Put it in the double-boiler with the cold milk, and place on the fire. Cook for twenty minutes, stirring frequently; then add the salt, and strain into a bowl. Now add the sugar and flavor. Rinse a bowl in cold water, and, after turning the blancmange into it, set it away to harden. Serve with powdered sugar and cream.[23]

Blancmange – if made with cream rather than milk and gelatine rather than arrowroot or Irish moss – is a lot like panna cotta, the famed jellied cream pudding of Italy's Piedmont region. Now popular throughout Italy and beyond, it is often served accompanied by pears or other fruits, just as Hannah Glasse served her blancmange. Green leaves and geraniums are lovely as well.

A SPOONFUL OF BLANCMANGE

Blancmange was considered a beneficial dish for the sick during the medieval era. Not only was it smooth and easily digested, but it was made with that valuable medicine, sugar. Chicken and almonds were also healthful, making blancmange perfect for balancing one's humours. The fourteenth-century recipe collection known as the *Viandier* included a *blanc mengier d'un chappon pour ung malade* (blancmange made with capon for the sick).[24]

Five centuries later, when humoral theory was no longer influential, blancmange was still medicinal, though it was no longer made with capons. Fannie Farmer's *Food and Cookery for the Sick and Convalescent* (1904) included two blancmange recipes, one chocolate and the other vanilla. Like her colleague Maria Parloa, she used Irish moss to thicken them. *Little Women*'s Meg March made blancmange for their neighbour Laurie when he was sick. Her sister Jo delivered it saying, 'It's so simple, you can eat it, and, being soft, it will slip down without hurting your sore throat.'[25]

CURDS AND WHEY

Little Miss Muffet
Sat on a tuffet
Eating her curds and whey.
Along came a spider
Who sat down beside her
And frightened Miss Muffet away.

In addition to making twenty-first-century children frightened of spiders, this traditional nursery rhyme raises some questions. 'What is a tuffet?' children ask. 'What are curds and whey?' And why was Little Miss Muffet eating such things? For parents, answering the first question is easy. The accompanying illustration usually helps. A tuffet is a low seat or small hassock. Sometimes called a pouffe, it is different from a plain stool because it is cloth-covered and usually padded or upholstered.

Curds and whey present a different challenge. To youngsters or the uninitiated, the phrase 'curds and whey' sounds like curdled milk – the milk left in the refrigerator before we go away on holiday that

In this 1884 painting by Sir John Everett Millais, pretty little Miss Muffet looks truly terrified by the spider.

greets us with a sour smell when we return. In a sense, that is true. But curds are one of the oldest dairy dishes and more akin to fresh cottage cheese or ricotta than milk gone bad. Curds are the solid parts of milk that form as a result of contact with rennet or an acid, usually during cheese-making. The whey is the thin, greenish milk that settles below. But curds and whey also were made and enjoyed on their own. To make them, one added rennet to fresh warm milk, which might be left plain or flavoured with lemon, rosewater, peach stones (for a bitter almond taste) or vanilla. After the rennet was added, the milk was left in a warm place until the curd rose to the top and the whey settled on the bottom.

Street vendors sold curds and whey in 18th-century London.

The rennet used to make cheese or curds and whey comes from the stomach of a calf, and pieces were purchased from the local butcher. Before being used, the piece of rennet had to be scoured, rubbed with salt and left to dry. Then boiling water was poured over it, and the rennet was left to steep for six hours or more. Finally, the rennet would be removed and the liquid that was left was added to the milk to turn it. Wine or lemon juice could also be used to curdle the milk, but they were not considered as effective as rennet. A recipe for 'runnet or trifle cream' used 'hartiechockes' in place of the rennet. Said to be the French way, they were believed to give the cream a more pleasant flavour.[26]

The curds and whey might have been sent to the table accompanied by a pitcher of cream or white wine, along with some sugar and nutmeg. Or the cook might skim off the curds and set them on a sieve to drain. Then she would sprinkle them with sugar and nutmeg and serve them in bowls, with cream poured over them. Similarly, today in Cyprus, where the famous halloumi cheese is made, some of the warm curds are scooped off and served topped with a sprinkling of orange-flower water and a swirl of carob syrup. Sitting in a garden on a sunny spring afternoon and eating curds and carob syrup is a treat Miss Muffet would have loved.

Whey was also drunk on its own. For years it was a simple summer drink for country folk. Also called 'whig', it became a fashionable health drink in the seventeenth and eighteenth centuries. In his diary, Samuel Pepys noted that he went to a 'whay-house' and drank 'a great deal of whay'. Drinking whey, known in France as *petit lait*, was reputed to have cured Madame de Pompadour's headaches and menstrual cramps.[27]

Curds, or soft fresh cheese, are also the basis for cheesecake. Cooks have drained curds, pounded them smooth and turned them into lush, creamy cheesecakes since ancient times. The Greek athletes who competed in the first Olympic Games in 776 BCE were served cakes containing cheese.[28] Cooks in eighteenth-century England flavoured their cheesecakes with lemon, rose- or orange-flower water or nutmeg, and sometimes added currants or plums to them. They poured the mixture into pastry-lined pie plates or small tart pans to bake. Today, wherever cheese is made, cheesecakes are enjoyed. They are traditionally associated with springtime holidays like Easter or Shavuot. New York cheesecake, made with cream cheese, is now considered a classic.

GOING ON A JUNKET

Another creamy pudding was called 'junket'. The word was derived from the French *jonquette*, meaning a rush basket in which cheese was shaped. The word came to be used for the cheese itself, and then for a sweetened and flavoured curd dessert. It was also a generic name for any sweetmeat or delicacy. Platina included a recipe for *jonchada de*

These junkets look much more appealing than the one Irving Cobb was served in the hospital.

amandole (almond junket) in *De honesta voluptate et valetudine.* He used almond milk in lieu of cow's milk for fasting days.[29]

During the sixteenth century, the word 'junket' came to be used to describe a merry feast or banquet. By the nineteenth, in the U.S., it had evolved to mean a trip taken by an official at the expense of the government and usually believed by taxpayers to be frivolous and wasteful. Junket, like blancmange and flummery, was considered a good sickroom dish. But not everyone enjoyed the bland version – sans whipped cream, rum, almonds or any other enhancements – that most patients would have received. Irving Cobb, an American writer who was a *Saturday Evening Post* correspondent during the First World War, wrote about his reaction to junket while he was in a hospital convalescing after surgery.

I know not how it may be in the world at large, but in a hospital, junket is a custard that by some subtle process has been denuded of those ingredients which make a custard fascinating and exciting. It tastes as though the eggs, which form its underlying basis, had been laid in a fit of pique by a hen that was severely upset at the time.[30]

SNOWSCAPES

From the sixteenth to the early nineteenth century, winters were often so cold that the era became known as the Little Ice Age. Europe and North America shivered as temperatures plunged. The weather frequently wreaked havoc on crops and trade, and many suffered – especially, as always, the poor. Farmers, fishermen and winemakers were just a few of those who saw their livelihoods diminished or destroyed. In England, the Thames, which was wider and shallower than it is today, often froze. When it did, Londoners took advantage of an opportunity to wrest enjoyment from the snow and ice and created impromptu 'frost fairs' on the frozen surface.

Children and adults alike skated, slipped and slid on the river of ice. Musicians played. Horse-drawn carriages took the place of boats and ferried passengers across the river. Merchants erected refreshment tents on the ice and sold everything from roast beef to gingerbread to hot chocolate. During the last of the frost fairs, in 1814, it was claimed that an elephant was paraded safely across the Thames. Printers set up their presses on the ice and made and sold souvenir flyers, many featuring humorous messages like this one:

NOTICE

Whereas you J. Frost have by Force and Violence taken possession of the River Thames, I hereby give you warning to Quit immediately.

A. Thaw

Printed by S. Warner on the Ice. Feb. 5, 1814.[31]

Perhaps the snow-frosted landscape outdoors inspired the wintry wonderlands that confectioners and cooks created indoors on their banquet tables. During the eighteenth century, cooks in fashionable households blanketed their tables with snowy sweets. They whipped cream and egg whites into frothy swirls and tucked sprigs of rosemary in them to resemble tiny trees atop snow-covered peaks. They dipped fruits in water and chilled them until they seemed covered with frost. They made all sorts of cooked creams and custard puddings and concocted creamy alcoholic drinks.

Joseph Addison (1672–1719), an English philosopher, connoisseur of beauty and essayist, was so delighted by one dessert display that he thought it was vulgar to destroy the effect by eating any of it, although others at the table had no such compunctions. Writing in *The Tatler*, on Tuesday, 21 March 1709, Addison described with great scorn

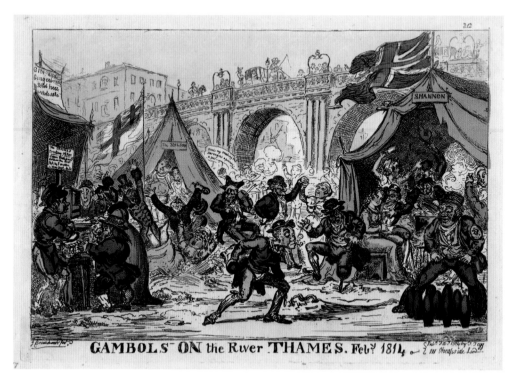

George Cruikshank's caricature of a riotous frost fair on the Thames, 1814.

a dinner that featured all manner of 'French kickshaws' (a corruption of the French *quelque chose*, or 'somethings'), which he did not care to eat, including something that looked liked 'roasted porcupine' but turned out to be larded turkey. Finally he spied 'the noble sirloin', which had been ignominiously banished to a side table, and partook. He was quite annoyed that the roast had taken second place to the 'dainties', but his mood brightened considerably when the desserts were displayed. He wrote,

> The dessert was brought up at last, which in truth was as extraordinary as any thing that had come before it. The whole, when ranged in its proper order, looked like a very beautiful winter-piece. There were several pyramids of candied sweetmeats, that hung like icicles, with fruits scattered up and down, and hid in an artificial kind of frost. At the same time there were great quantities of cream beaten up into a snow, and near them little plates of sugar-plums, disposed like so many heaps of hail-stones, with a multitude of congelations in jellies of various colours. I was indeed so pleased with the several objects which lay before me, that I did not care for displacing any of them; and was half angry with the rest of the company, that, for the sake of a piece of lemon-peel, or a sugar-plum, would spoil so pleasing a picture.[32]

The tables must have looked as lovely and tranquil as a silent, snow-covered garden. The enormous amount of work that went into creating such a setting went on below stairs, where most of the guests would never see it. Most home cooks would not have been able to create dazzling snowscapes on their dessert tables; but they did make snows, creams and custard puddings and garnish them prettily. In fact, various creams and snows had been made for centuries. Bartolomeo Scappi gave a sixteenth-century recipe for *neve di latte*, or milk snow. The *Proper New Booke of Cookery* (1545) includes a recipe titled 'To

Make a Dish Full of Snow' that is very similar to this one from Hannah
Woolley's cookbook *The Queen-like Closet or Rich Cabinet* (1672).[33]

TO MAKE SNOW CREAM

Take a Pint of Cream, and the Whites of three Eggs, one spoonful
or two of Rosewater, whip it to a Froth with a Birchen Rod, then
cast it off the Rod into a Dish, in the which you have first fastened
half a Manchet with some Butter on the bottom, and a long
Rosemary sprig in the middle; when you have all cast the Snow
on the dish, then garnish it with several sorts of sweet-meats.[34]

There are many similar recipes in other English as well as French
and German cookbooks. The 'manchet' she piled the snow on is a
small loaf of white bread; usually the crusts were removed before
the snow was swirled over the loaf. Some swirled their snow atop
apples instead. As they beat the cream and egg whites, they took off
the froth that rose up and piled it onto the bread or apple. Then
they repeated the process until the dish was full. In making some
other creams, they set each layer of froth on a sieve to dry, and then
whipped the remaining cream again, scooped again and continued
until all the cream was used.

Since cooks did not yet have wire whisks or rotary egg beaters
– much less our electric mixers – whipping cream and egg whites was
a laborious task. Cooks would use bunches of twigs tied together
and, as a result, recipes generally specify whipping the mixtures for
half an hour or more. The tedious effort did not prevent cooks from
adding creative touches to their work. Many made their whisks from
rosemary branches or tied a sprig of rosemary to the twigs to add flavour to their mixtures. Hannah Glasse tied lemon peel to hers, as did
many others. Some used peach tree twigs to impart a bitter-almond
flavour. In place of twigs, some used a *molinillo*, or chocolate mill –
the stirring tool from Mexico designed to froth hot chocolate – to
whip cream.

The term 'whipped cream' does not seem to have been used until the seventeenth century. In France, it was called *crème Chantilly* or *crème fouettée*. In Italy, whipped cream is *panna montata*; in Spain, *nata montada*; and in Germany, *Schlagsahne*. The Viennese, who are particularly fond of whipped cream, call it *Schlagobers*. The word was also the name of a ballet composed by Richard Strauss and choreographed by Heinrich Kröller – it was set in a Viennese cake shop, or *Konditorei*, where marzipan, gingerbread and fruitcakes came to life and danced. After *Schlagobers's* premiere in 1924, a critic named Heinrich Kralik wrote, 'This whipped-cream morsel is, however, not so easy to digest.'[35]

A cream that is cooked rather than whipped, called clotted cream, is still an English speciality, and has a close relative in the Near Eastern *kaymak*. Clotted cream, also known as Devonshire cream, is made by cooking milk or cream over very low heat and then letting it stand until it has set or clotted and carefully skimming off the thick cream layer. Most often it is eaten with scones, but it can also be a topping for fruit or simply eaten on its own. Hannah Woolley made a decorative dish called 'cabbage cream' by skimming off layers of clotted cream and arranging them to look like the leaves of a cabbage. Her recipe specified that a mixture of rosewater and sugar be spread between each layer to ensure that the petals did not stick together but retained the shape of a head of cabbage.

TO MAKE CABBAGE CREAM

Take twenty five Quarts of new Milk, set it on the fire till it be ready to boil, stir it all the while that it creams not, then pour it into twenty several Platters so fast as you can, when it is cold, take off the Cream with a Skimmer, and lay it on a Pie Plate in the fashion of a Cabbage, crumpled one upon another, do thus three times, and between every Layer you must mingle Rosewater and Sugar mingled thick, and laid on with a Feather; some use to take a little Cream and boil it with Ginger, then take it from the fire and season it with

Rosewater and Sugar, and the Juice of Jordan Almonds blanched and beaten, then stir it till it be cold, that it cream not; then take Toasts of Manchet cut thin, not too hard, nor brown, lay them in the bottom of the Dish, and pour the Cream upon them, and lay the Cabbage over.[36]

A Charming Confusion

Defining some of these dairy desserts and tracing their histories is a challenge. Recipes vary considerably, and one cook's fool was another's trifle. Fools, usually defined as a simple mixture of cream and fruits such as gooseberries or rhubarb today, once resembled the more complex layered combination of cake, custard, wine and whipped cream (at a minimum) that came to be known as a trifle. Both are at once rich and simple, frothy and fanciful. Neither name is intended to be pejorative. Rather they suggest desserts that are light and ephemeral, made up primarily of wispy clouds of cream. Their definitions are as intangible as the desserts themselves. The *Oxford English Dictionary* defines a fool as 'a dish composed of cream boiled with various ingredients', and calls it 'obscure'. The OED then cites this as the earliest usage: 'a kinde of clouted cream called a foole or a trifle in English', from John Florio's *A Worlde of Wordes; or, Most Copious, and Exact Dictionarie in English and Italian* (1598).[37] So we have a late sixteenth-century reference that conflates clotted cream, fool and trifle. It is true that most early recipes for trifles do not result in the many-layered wonders we know as trifles today. They are more like classic fools – fruits swirled into whipped cream and served as a lush, light summer dessert. At the same time, early recipes for fools sometimes call for custard rather than simple whipped cream and some add biscuits or cakes as well, making them more closely resemble today's trifle. Randle Holme, author of *The Academy of Armory*, written nearly a century after Florio's work, in 1688, wrote, 'Foole is a kind of Custard, but more crudely; being made of Cream, Yolks of Eggs, Cinamon, Mace

Today's elegant
coronation trifle.

boiled: and served on Sippets with sliced Dates, Sugar, and white and
red Comfits, strawed thereon.'[38] Sippets were small, neatly cut pieces
of bread, making this closer to a trifle than a fool.

Today, most define a fool as a simple mixture of sweetened, puréed
fruit and cream, and nothing else. Gooseberries have always been one
of the most popular fool fruits. This recipe, from a nineteenth-century

American cookbook compiled by Estelle Woods Wilcox, offers the cook a choice between combining the fruit with a custard or simply with cream:

GOOSEBERRY FOOL
Stew gooseberries until soft, add sugar, and press through
a colander (earthen is best), then make a boiled custard, or
sweeten enough rich cream (about one gill to each quart), and
stir carefully into the gooseberries just before sending to table.
– Mrs. L. S. W.[39]

Today's trifle has many variations, but essentially it is a cake or biscuit base soaked in a liquor, topped with custard, and possibly jelly, and crowned with syllabub or whipped cream. In his late nineteenth-century novel *Elsie Venner: A Romance of Destiny*, the American author Oliver Wendell Holmes described it as 'that most wonderful object of domestic art called *trifle* . . . with its charming confusion of cream and cake and almonds and jam and jelly and wine and cinnamon and froth.'[40]

Trifles travelled quite naturally from Britain to other English-speaking countries, including the United States, Australia, New Zealand, India during the Raj and Anglophone Canada. They also found their way to other nations. In their book *Trifle*, writers Helen Saberi and Alan Davidson traced it to France, where culinary writer Jules Gouffé named it *mousse a l'anglaise*, as well as to Germany, Iceland, Hungary, Eritrea, South Africa and Russia.[41]

Amelia Simmons, author of the first truly American cook-book, made a simple trifle. Her book is generally known as *American Cookery*; however, its full title was *American Cookery; or, The Art of Dressing Viands, Fish, Poultry and Vegetables, and the Best Modes of Making Pastes, Puffs, Pies, Tarts, Puddings, Custards and Preserves, and all kinds of Cakes From the Imperial Plumb to Plain Cake, Adapted to This Country, and all Grades of Life.* English and other cookbooks were printed in or brought to America, but hers was the first both written and published there. Published in 1796, the book is famed for its inclusion of American ingredients, such as cranberries, using watermelon rind to make 'American citron' and using the American word 'molasses' rather than the English 'treacle'. Her recipe for trifle was similar to English ones of the same era, but hers is more down-to-earth and pithy than most:

A TRIFLE

Fill a dish with biscuit finely broken, rusk, and spiced cake, wet with wine, then pour a good boil'd custard, (not too thick) over the rusk, and put a syllabub over that; garnish with jelley and flowers.[42]

Italians make a similar dessert called *zuppa inglese*. Saberi and Davidson called it 'an Italian dessert which is related in composition (sponge cake/biscuits, liqueur, custard and/or cream, optional topping/decoration), although not necessarily in ancestry, to the English trifle'.[43] However, in the 1891 English-language edition of *La scienza in cucina e l'arte di mangiar bene*, titled *Science in the Kitchen and the Art of Eating Well*, Pellegrino Artusi called his recipe 'Zuppa Inglese (English trifle)'. The more baroque Sicilian version is called *cassata* or *cassata palermitana*. There are as many versions as cooks who make it, but in general it is a sponge cake doused with a liqueur, layered with a filling of ricotta, candied fruit and possibly chocolate, and covered with a sugar frosting and/or marzipan or, less often, whipped cream. Tiramisu, a twentieth-century dessert that consists of layers of espresso-and-rum-soaked ladyfingers, creamy zabaglione and mascarpone filling, and whipped cream, is a close relative as well. Perhaps the best-known and most-loved creamy ricotta dessert is Sicily's *cannoli*. Their delicately sweetened ricotta filling, often enhanced with bits of chocolate or candied citron or pumpkin, is encased in a cylinder of crisp pastry. The open ends may be sprinkled with finely chopped pistachios. When filled at the last minute to prevent sogginess, they are a perfect blend of cream and crunch.

Another twentieth-century relation is Latin America's *pastel de tres leches* (three milks cake). A sponge cake soaked in a mixture of condensed milk, evaporated milk and cream, the recipe was likely developed by Nestlé in the 1970s or '80s. It is most associated with Mexico, but nearly every Latin American country has its own version.[44]

QUIVERING, COWARDLY CUSTARDS

Custards of one sort or another date back to at least the fourteenth century. The word 'custard' was derived from *crustade*, meaning a tart with a crust. It was usually an open pie containing meat or fruit as well as a preparation of broth or milk, eggs and spices. Whether savoury or sweet, it was served within the meal rather than at its end. Eventually it became a favourite in the dessert course, while still being enjoyed as a savoury quiche.

Sweet custards – the mixture of milk, eggs, sugar and a flavouring cooked to a creamy consistency – are among the most versatile kitchen creations. They may be softly simmered on a stovetop, oven-baked, *brûléed*, baked and served on their own in plain cups, moulded into decorative shapes, baked in pies or tarts, used as a filling for choux pastries like éclairs or cream puffs, served as a sauce, flavoured with anything from vanilla to peach leaves, and even breaded and fried. Custard forms the sea that France's *île flottante* floats on. Frozen, custard becomes ice cream.

Custards and their variations are called puddings, creams, *crèmes*, crèmes anglaises, crème caramel, pastry creams and flans. The French kitchen vocabulary uses the word *crème*, rather than custard. In Spain, it is *natilla*; in Italy, *crema*; in Germany, *Vanillepudding*; in Portugal, *creme de ovos*. In Thailand and Laos, custards called *sangkaya* are made with coconut milk and cooked in containers carved from young, soft coconuts or in a hollowed-out squash or pumpkin.

Set of Spode lidded custard cups and stand, *c.* 1810, in Lattice Scroll pattern.

Custards baked into pies and tarts are ubiquitous. Scappi's sixteenth-century custard pie, *pasticci di latte*, was flavoured with rose-water and cinnamon. The individual Portuguese custard pastries called *pastéis de nata* are usually flavoured with cinnamon and are famed throughout the Portuguese-speaking world from Portugal to Brazil to Macau and beyond. Coconut custard and banana cream pies were once highlights of American diner menus.

Custards also inspire humour. In a seventeenth-century essay titled 'The Cook', the author and Anglican clergyman John Earle portrayed the cook as a violent man who waged war in his kitchen using such weapons as sharp knives and scalding water. The cook, according to Earle, ranged his dishes in military order with strong and hardy meats in the forefront, 'and the more cold and cowardly in the rear; as quaking tarts and quivering custards, and such milk-sop dishes'.[45] In the early twentieth century, quivering custard pies prepared with especially soft fillings appeared in nearly every slapstick film in Hollywood. Tossing a pie at someone and watching it splatter all over the victim's face was considered the height of hilarity. It was such a popular gag in 1920s Hollywood that the pastry shop that supplied them to Keystone Studios made nothing else.[46]

Chefs get set to toss in the 1947 film *The Perils of Pauline*.

Sight gags, sickroom dishes, simple homespun desserts, pastry chefs' sumptuous creations – creams and custards are all of these. They are also the basis of ice cream, which replaced them in popularity when ice became available to all. At least one person lamented the absence of the earlier desserts. In an 1891 article titled 'Syllabub and Syllabub-vessels', Henry Syer Cuming, a collector who founded the Cuming Museum in London, wrote that syllabubs and the vessels made for them were in danger of passing into oblivion. He noted that the serving vessels were rare by then and those who were fortunate enough to have them should cherish them. He also offered this curious verse.

WHIPT SYLLABUB

When syllabub like mount of snow,
With custard, jelly, tart,
And tipsy cake, and trifle sweet,
Of banquet made a part.
O! syllabub was our delight,
Enriched with spice and sack:
Ah! then we loved to taste the whip
In mouth, not on the back.
What hubbub did the children raise
At sight of syllabub!
Their mouths did water for its foam.
With glee they palms did rub.
Tho silly folk hath now forgot
How syllabub was made,
And fancy that to Scilly Isles

Nearly every culture has its own version, but no matter what it's called, the combination of cream and caramel is a perfect flavour marriage.

Afresh must seek for aid.
O! sure their brains must addled be
By craft of Belzebub,
Whose cruel spite would them deprive
Of joy of syllabub.[47]

Cuming was correct in believing that syllabubs – as well as curds and whey, possets, leaches, snows and flummeries – were seldom encountered by then.[48] Why settle for such old-fashioned dishes when one could have ice cream? At the turn of the twentieth century, the joy of ice cream was our delight.

FOUR

THE PROSE AND POETRY OF DESSERT

'THERE IS POETRY IN DESSERT,' wrote Mrs Beeton, and certainly the lofty snows, flummery fish and cabbage creams that were featured on dessert tables justify her description.[1] But as she well knew, there was also much prose in dessert. It was not easy to make desserts when eggs or batter had to be mixed for an hour with nothing but a bunch of twigs. Or when someone had to carry heavy loads of wood or coal to fuel the stove before baking could begin. Making ice cream was impossible without a supply of ice, and difficult even with one. The number and variety of desserts were limited to those that could be prepared with the existing tools and the ingredients that were available or affordable. Generally, that meant the making of desserts was the responsibility of servants, and enjoying them was limited to the well-off. But during the nineteenth century, scientific discoveries as well as improvements in equipment, manufacturing and transportation resulted in easier-to-make, less expensive desserts, and many more of them.

When it was new, ice cream was so exclusive that just one dish of it was served at the banquet course of the 1671 Feast of the Garter. No one but King Charles II had a taste. It took centuries to put ice cream on the everyday dessert table. But by the nineteenth century, with an ice industry, new ice-cream churns and cheap sugar, street urchins in cities in England and America could buy ice cream for as little as a penny.

S 1. Jelly of two colours.   T 1. Raspberry Cream.   U 1. Centre Dish of various Fruits
V 1. Trifle.   W 1. Strawberries au naturel in ornamental Flowerpot.

Mrs Beeton presented her jellies, creams, trifle and fruit desserts
in simple but elegant style.

During the sixteenth century, Neapolitan alchemists experimenting with freezing discovered that adding salt or saltpetre to snow or
ice enabled them to freeze other substances. Initially, cooks used the
new freezing technique to freeze fruits and flowers in water-filled,
pyramid-shaped moulds, which decorated dinner tables and cooled
the air. They dipped fruits in water, froze them until they gleamed
and displayed them. They set marzipan boats afloat on icy seas. But it
was not until the late seventeenth century that cooks learned how to
apply the technique of freezing to drinks and creams. When they did,
they turned the *sorbetto* Florio had defined in his 1611 dictionary – 'a
kind of drink used in Turkie made of water and juice of Limonds,
Sugar, Amber, and Muske, very costly and delicate' – into frozen sorbets.[2] Cooks transformed the many then-popular creams and custard
puddings into ice creams or, as they were originally called, 'iced creams'
and 'iced puddings'.

Antonio Latini was the *scalco*, or steward, in charge of the
household of a Spanish noble in Naples when his late seventeenth-
century work *Lo scalco alla moderna* (The Modern Steward) was
published. It was one of the first books to provide recipes for making
ices and ice creams. Latini used the words *sorbetto/sorbetti* for both
ices made with fruit juices and those made with cream. The word
gelato was not used until the nineteenth century. Latini wrote that
great quantities of *sorbetti* were eaten in Naples, and that every Neapolitan was born knowing how to make them. That was no doubt an
exaggeration, especially because he pointed out that making them
was best left to professionals. His recipes were not detailed. Unless
one knew the techniques, it would be difficult to learn how to make
ice cream from his book. However, his flavours were fascinating.
They included a *sorbetto di latte*, or milk ice, flavoured with candied
citron or pumpkin. He added pine nuts to a cinnamon ice. He made
a sour cherry ice with fresh cherries and another using dried cherries
when fresh ones were not in season. He had two recipes for chocolate
sorbetti, an innovative use of chocolate at a time when it was more

often simply a drink. He called one of his chocolate *sorbetti* a frozen mousse and said it should be stirred constantly during the freezing process. It was his only mention of the need to stir the mixtures, a necessity future cooks would emphasize. Latini also pointed out that ices should have the consistency of sugar and snow; that is, they should not be hard and icy.

A limited number of ice-cream recipes were published in cookbooks in subsequent years. Generally, they were more descriptive of the freezing techniques than the make-up of the cream. Mrs Glasse and Mrs Raffald had similar recipes. This is Mrs Raffald's:

> Pare, stone, and scald twelve ripe apricots, beat them
> in a fine marble mortar. Put to them six ounces of
> double-refined sugar, a pint of scalding cream, work
> it through a hair sieve. Put it into a tin that has a close
> cover, set it in a tub of ice broken small and a large
> quantity of salt put amongst it. When you see your
> cream grow thick round the edges of your tin, stir it,
> and set it in again till it all grows quite thick. When
> your cream is all froze up, take it out of your tin and
> put it in the mould you intend it to be turned out of,
> then put on the lid. Have ready another tub with ice
> and salt in as before, put your mould in the middle and
> lay your ice under and over it, let it stand four or five
> hours. Dip your tin in warm water when you turn it out.
> If it be summer you must not turn it out till the moment
> you want it. You may use any sort of fruit if you have not
> apricots, only observe to work it fine.[3]

Finally, in 1768, *L'Art de bien faire les glaces d'office* (The Art of Making Ices for the Confectionery Kitchen) was published in Paris. It was the first book completely devoted to making ices and ice creams. Written by M. Emy, a confectioner about whom we know little except that he was highly skilled, it included more than one hundred recipes, along with directions on freezing, moulding and serving. Emy wrote for professional confectioners. His instructions were explicit, and he said that if they were followed carefully, the ice cream would be *parfait*. His flavours rivalled those of today's most adventurous pastry chefs – ambergris, rye bread, pineapple, white coffee, Parmesan and Gruyère, truffle (the fungus), vanilla and many more.

Emy was a perfectionist, but also a pragmatist. He believed it was better to use fruits and berries in season, both for their taste and for the pleasure of anticipation. In winter when fresh fruits were unavailable, he recommended making ice creams with chocolate, coffee, cinnamon or other spices instead. But he explained how to make ice creams with preserved fruits because he knew that confectioners' employers would demand fruit-flavoured ice creams even in winter. He also disapproved of using alcohol in ices and ice creams, but offered advice on which ones to use if required to do so. He thought maraschino liqueur, rum or the cordial *ratafia* would do, but said that he would not answer for their quality.[4]

Emy and other confectioners moulded and coloured ice creams to resemble the same sorts of fruits, vegetables, flowers and other fanciful shapes earlier made from flummeries, leaches, jellies and creams. They moulded ice cream into trompe l'oeil fish, like Mrs Eales's trout cream. They made ice-cream melons, pears, pickles, swans, fish, hams and more. Some confectioners were so skilled at making disguised ices that occasionally they fooled diners. When guests discovered that the various fruits, meats and fish were actually ice creams, most were impressed and delighted. The joke is reminiscent of the sugar banquet that fooled, and delighted, Henry of Valois.

Similar ice-cream antics flourished over time. In *The Thorough Good Cook* (1895), author George Sala noted that he had seen astonishing ice creams in Vienna. He wrote, 'They will send you up ices simulating with marvellous closeness lobsters, oysters, bundles of asparagus, and even mutton cutlets and small hams.' One year, when he was hosting a dinner for some friends, he decided to try 'a cream-ice surprise' of his own. He had several large potatoes baked until their skins were 'corrugated rather than smooth'. After cutting the potatoes in half, scooping out the insides, and brushing them with egg white, he had them filled with ice cream. Then he joined the halves together and served the 'praties' on a napkin on a dish. He listed them on the menu as 'baked potatoes à la tin can'. According to Sala, most of his guests were deceived. One said, 'Shocking!' Another said, 'I could not possibly.' But one man winked, took one, opened it up and revealed the treat within. When asked how he knew, he replied: 'Baked potatoes

As practical as it was beautiful, this Sèvres ice-cream server from 1778 held ice both inside the pail and in the recessed cover to keep the contents cold. A compartment inside held the ice cream itself.

In 1805 in Paris, eating ice cream could be a posh affair.

. . . are not served cold; and the guests, when potatoes come round, do not have glass plates with ice spoons set before them.'[5]

DESSERT FOR EVERYONE

The Industrial Revolution, as it spread from the UK to Germany, France, the U.S. and other countries, created profound changes in people's lives, both positive and negative. Numbered among the positive changes was making ice, and in turn ice cream, affordable for ordinary people. In the eighteenth century, the well-to-do might have access to ice from a pond or lake and have an ice house in which to

---

SMALL MOULDS and FORCING PIPES.

No. 205.
COPPER EGG.

No. 217B.
SWAN MOULD.

No. 208A.
COPPER
BALLETTE MOULD.

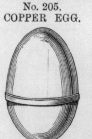

15s. per doz.

12s. per doz.

15s. per doz.

No. 220.
ROSE
FORCING
PIPE.

No. 201.
CORNET TINS.

No. 222.
PLAIN
FORCING PIPE.

6d. each.

2s. 6d. per doz.

6d. each.
3 sizes of Mouth,
$\frac{1}{8}$, $\frac{1}{4}$, and $\frac{1}{2}$ inch.

No. 223A.   ARTICHOKE.

No. 221.   VINE LEAF.

New Design (Registered), 1$\frac{3}{4}$ in. diam.
10s. per doz.

3s. per doz.

Mrs Agnes Marshall advertised her ice-cream moulds in her 1894 book *Fancy Ices*.

At any age, ice cream is a special treat.

store it. It was not until the mid-nineteenth century, when an American, Frederic Tudor, turned harvesting, storing, delivering and selling ice into a worldwide business, that ice became available to nearly everyone. Tudor and later his competitors made ice a commodity. It was shipped to countries around the world and delivered from door to door. Iceboxes that held blocks of ice and stored cold foods became common household appliances. The availability of ice had a far-reaching impact. Food distribution changed as ice-cooled railroad cars allowed fresh fruits, vegetables, fish and freshly slaughtered meats to travel long distances to new markets. Ice changed medical practice when it was used to treat feverish patients. And easy access to ice made the production and sale of ice cream practical.

When Tudor shipped ice from Boston to Calcutta, India's ice-cream business began. Today throughout India, people enjoy ice-cream flavours like mango, pistachio and fig along with chocolate-coated 'chocobars' that children love. The country's traditional frozen dessert is called *kulfi*. It is made by cooking milk until it caramelizes, and then adding sugar, pistachios, almonds and rose water. Unlike ice cream, the mixture is frozen without churning and shaped in conical moulds.[6]

In 1843 Nancy Johnson, an American woman from Philadelphia, invented the first ice-cream freezer with a built-in churn turned by an outer crank. Her freezer eliminated the need to open the container to stir the ice-cream mixture and made the freezing process faster and easier for professionals and home cooks alike. It mixed the ice cream to the smooth consistency confectioners like Emy had long recommended, and it also gave young boys, who were often enlisted with the chore of turning the crank, the reward of licking the paddle. In England, confectioner Thomas Masters invented a similar ice-cream freezer in 1844. His could also be used to produce ice, and he was one of the first to make ice cream with artificially made ice. But since natural ice was available by then and considered safer, his device had little success.

Eventually others improved on the early inventions and, by the latter half of the nineteenth century, ice-cream makers for both home and professional use were widespread. Trade publications advertised ice-cream makers run by horsepower, and then steam power, for use in hotels, restaurants, ice-cream parlours and confectioners' shops. Even in Italy, where ice cream was a source of national pride, the foreign ice-cream-making equipment was prized. In *Science in the Kitchen and the Art of Eating Well*, Pellegrino Artusi wrote,

Street vendors of ice cream were looked down upon by elite confectioners, but children loved their wares.

Thanks to the American ice cream makers, which have triple action and need no spatula, making ice cream has become so much easier and faster that it would be a shame not to enjoy much more frequently the sensual pleasure of this delicious food.[7]

With the new equipment and access to ice, everyone from home cooks to street vendors began making ice cream, much to the chagrin of elite professional confectioners and other traditionalists. Andrew Tuer, author of *Old London Street Cries* (1885), was sceptical of the quality of the penny ices called 'Hokey-pokey' peddled by street vendors. He described them as 'dreadfully sweet, dreadfully cold, and hard as a brick. It is whispered that the not unwholesome Swede turnip, crushed into pulp, has been known to form its base, in lieu of more expensive supplies from the cow'.[8] The British confectioner Frederick T. Vine characterized the street-vendors' ices as 'questionable'.[9] The American editor of an 1883 edition of the *Confectioners' Journal* was more hostile. He described the ice creams made by 'slop-shop, Cheap-John-Factorymen's processes' as

Customers licked ice cream from the glass called a 'penny lick' and then returned it to the vendor. It might, or might not, be washed after each use.

the fraudulent and depraved wares of the factories, pinch-back creams, church fair and charity creams, boarding-house and almshouse creams, which are no creams but only frothy, water slop and slush and still viler 'flavorings,' whose make up is only known to the devil's chemical emissaries.[10]

However, these critics were on the wrong side of history. Ice cream was everywhere, and people everywhere loved it. In 1891 the steamship *Hamburg American Packet* made a voyage around the world with ice cream in its hold and on its menu. Thereafter, steamship dessert menus always featured ice cream, as did railroad dining cars, hotels, restaurants and American drugstore soda fountains, often pairing it with cake or pie. Ice cream was made by home cooks and confectioners, sold on the street, enjoyed in ice-cream parlours and served to the great and the small.

Colour plates enhance the look of Gouffé's pastries in the 1893 edition of his work, which was published in Rotterdam.

FROM CASTLE TO COTTAGE

The Pastry-cook's art is appreciated in all civilised lands, and its origin dates from the infancy of the world, namely, from the day when man having before him flour, butter, and eggs, must have been led to combine them in different ways to flatter the palate. Hence cakes and *brioche*.

By degrees he added honey, sugar, and fruits; he shaped these preparations in the most diverse ways, and ultimately, from the cottage to the castle, the traditional cake graced the festive board on all high days and holidays.[11]

Jules Gouffé, a prominent French chef, wrote this abbreviated history of cake-making as part of the introduction to his confectionery cookbook. He also noted that in earlier times,

PLAAT II.

VERSCHILLENDE GEBAKKEN.
1. Brioche. — 2. Manqué. — 3. Timbale van amandeldeeg gevuld met room en aardbeien. —
4. Croquembouche van genueesch gebak. — 5. Parijsche Nougat. — 6. Biscuit.
7. Sultane. — 8. Breton.

a knowledge of the elements of pastry formed no unimportant part of the female training; noble ladies, the daughters of wealthy citizens, recluses in their convents, could all use their hands to good purpose in the preparation of manifold choice delicacies.[12]

He said his book was intended for such women as much as for professional male pastry chefs.

Gouffé was correct in saying that man – and woman – began experimenting with cakes and other sweet dishes in ancient times. But he overlooked the role industrialization played in democratizing desserts, from ice cream to cake. During the nineteenth century, new ovens, utensils, moulds, leaveners, ingredients, transportation and refrigeration all changed the repertoire of the pastry and dessert cook, whether professional or amateur. New cookbooks also had an impact. At the time, cookbooks, especially those directed at the expanding middle class, proliferated. Some even included colour illustrations. The books not only featured recipes, but offered advice on how to organize a dinner party, garnish dishes and set a fashionable table. Many were written by women for women, but some male chefs wrote cookbooks intended to be used by women as well as professional cooks, who were assumed to be male. All of the new developments transformed baking, and cooks began creating a dizzying array of desserts.

EASIER BAKE OVENS

Just as new equipment and supplies had simplified ice-cream-making and made it more affordable, new ovens improved baking as well. Once cooks became accustomed to them, the new ovens were easier to use and more efficient than those of the past. The cast-iron wood or coal-burning stoves that were in use in the Netherlands, the UK and the U.S. during the early nineteenth century made baking easier, but they still necessitated stoking the oven with heavy loads of coal or wood. Then, in 1826, the English inventor James Sharp was awarded a patent for a gas stove. Many cities were beginning to become illuminated with gas lamps, and so families in urban areas began out-fitting their kitchens with the new gas stoves. Some resisted, as some resist every new technology, but Alexis Soyer, the celebrity chef at London's exclusive Reform Club, recommended them, which likely hastened their acceptance. He wrote:

> The gas stoves also tend to greater economy, as they are not lit til the moment wanted, then only the quantity required, and may be put out the moment it is done with. I think it a great pity that they can only be fitted in London and other large towns daily supplied with gas, but it is there it is most required, as the kitchens are smaller than in country houses, no heat whatever being created in the smallest kitchens by the use of gas stoves.[13]

Soyer did not mention it, but home cooks especially must have appreciated not having to carry loads of wood or coal for the ovens, as well as the improved cleanliness of their kitchens. By the early part

This 1870 advertisement for a new stove suggested that it was so easy to use, even children could bake with it.

of the twentieth century, as more cities added electricity, electric stoves also came to be used. Thermostats were finally included in both gas and electric ovens by then, although the technology had been experimented with and used for many years.

Before such ovens and controllable heat, cooks relied on their judgement and experience to tell them when an oven was ready for baking and how long to bake various foods. Recipes used such terms as a slack oven, or a quick oven, or a brisk oven. Some cooks judged an oven's heat by putting their hand in to see how long they could hold it there. Or they might hold a piece of white paper in the oven to see how long it took to brown. Describing the baking of cheesecakes, Raffald wrote that an oven that was too hot burns them and 'takes off their beauty', while 'a very slow oven makes them sad'.[14]

For a dessert of baked pears, the English cookbook author Eliza Acton advised putting them in the oven 'after the bread is drawn' and letting them remain all night. She said they would be 'much finer in flavour than those stewed or baked with sugar'.[15] The bread would have required a hotter oven; as it cooled off, it would be the right temperature for slowly baking the pears. In the introduction to her section on cakes, Acton wrote,

> All light cakes require a rather brisk oven to raise and set them;
> very large rich ones a well-sustained degree of heat sufficient to
> bake them through; and small sugar-cakes a very small oven,
> to prevent their taking a deep colour before they are half done:
> gingerbread too should be gently baked, unless it be of the light
> thick kind. Meringues, macaroons, and ratafias, will bear a slight
> degree more of heat than these.[16]

As late as 1904, in a book titled *German National Cookery for American Kitchens*, which was published in German as well as English, author Henriette Davidis suggested using paper to judge oven heat, offering this advice:

The degree of heat in the oven can be tested by means of a piece of paper. If the paper soon turns to a yellow (not black) color in the oven, this indicates the *first* degree of heat and is sufficient for puff paste and yeast dough; if it turns yellow slowly it indicates the *second* degree of heat, fit for most kinds of baking; the *third* degree must be still lower for cakes, etc., that should dry more than bake.[17]

By the turn of the century, some ovens had thermostats and books had begun to specify baking temperatures. Some recipes in an English confectioners' trade publication of 1904, called *The Book of Cakes*, specified oven temperatures of 300, 350 or 375° Fahrenheit (150, 175, 190° Celsius). Other recipes simply said 'bake'. An advertisement in the book for a 'New Patent Gas Oven' claimed that its gas supply was 'fully under control; heat can be regulated to a nicety'.[18]

In the twenty-first century, some cooks reverted to an early method when grilling over charcoal. Writing in an article in the 26 June 2016 edition of the *New York Times Magazine*, Sam Sifton recommended putting chicken on the grill when the coals were covered with gray ash and the temperature was medium. To judge it, he wrote, 'you can hold your hand 5 inches above the coals for 5 to 7 seconds'.[19]

TOOLS OF THE TRADE

In addition to the new ovens, cooks had new utensils. Wire whisks and mechanical egg beaters, as simple as they seem today, were a giant leap forward for cooks. When it was no longer necessary to beat eggs or batter for an hour or more with a bunch of twigs, baking cakes and biscuits and making meringues and other desserts became more practical and easier on the wrists. Several different types of mechanical beater were patented in the mid-nineteenth century, but one brand, Dover, became the best known. In the U.S., it was so popular that recipes often directed the cook to 'beat five minutes with "the Dover"'.[20]

English and European cooks did not take to the egg beater with the enthusiasm of the Americans and were more apt to use the wire whisk. It seems that no one clung to the use of bunches of twigs.

Cooks also had better means of measurement. Until the late nineteenth century, when measuring cups and spoons came onto the market, many recipes used measuring terms such as a tea cup or wine glass full of a liquid or a saltspoonful of a dry ingredient. They used such monetary terms as a pennyworth of a spice, or 'as much ground cinnamon as will cover a threepenny piece'.[21] Soyer directed his readers to roll pastry to the thickness of a halfpenny or half-crown, depending on the dish. He cut one pastry dough into twenty pieces, each 'rather larger than a penny-piece'.[22] Often, rather than calling for a specific amount of sugar, recipes simply directed the cook to sweeten to taste. Some called for 'enough' of an ingredient. It was up to the cook to be able to judge how much was enough.

European cooks came to use the more accurate weight rather than volume as a measurement. But for most Americans, measuring cups and spoons rather than scales replaced wine glasses and handfuls. Nineteenth-century American recipes for 'cup cakes' often meant cakes made according to a simple one-, two-, three-, four-cup formula – for example, one cup of butter, two cups of sugar, three cups of flour and four eggs, along with one teaspoonful of baking powder – rather than small cakes. American cookbooks, such as Fannie Merritt Farmer's popular *Boston Cooking-School Cook Book* (1896), insisted on accurate, level measurements and influenced the move away from weight to volume measurements. Europeans and Americans still differ in the same way, but today some recipe writers include both weight and volume measurements in their recipes so cooks can choose the option that suits them best.

Using an eggbeater was easier and faster than whisking with a bunch of twigs.

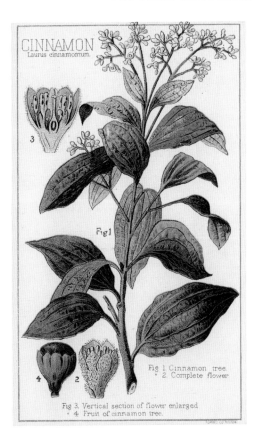

A 19th-century spice dealer's trade card illustrating cinnamon, one of the spices Europeans had travelled the world to obtain.

Cooks with years of experience might not have needed specific temperatures to gauge the heat of the oven or standardized measuring equipment, but young cooks often did, particularly if they had moved far from their families. With no one to guide them, they became a ready market for the new, easy-to-use baking products and instant mixes that were beginning to be manufactured.

ALL RISE

In 1790 the first U.S. patent, which was signed by George Washington, was granted to Samuel Hopkins for a process in the making of potash, an early form of leavening. Cooks had long used yeast to lighten cakes as well as to make breads, and they used beaten egg whites to make sponge cakes rise. Beating butter and sugar, called the creaming method, also helps cakes rise. Amelia Simmons used a leavening agent called 'pearl ash' (potassium bicarbonate), which was made from wood ashes, or 'emptins', an American term for a homemade liquid leavening made from hops or potatoes. But the commercially made chemical leaveners that were introduced in the mid-nineteenth century gave rise to the enormous increase in cake baking in the late nineteenth and early twentieth centuries.

Alfred Bird, the British chemist and founder of Bird and Sons Ltd., began experimenting with alternatives to yeast because his wife could not digest live yeasts. In 1843 he developed 'Bird's Fermenting Powder', later known as baking powder, and he soon produced the product commercially. He also created custard and blancmange

"PASTRY AND SWEETS."

The New and Enlarged Edition of this valuable little work, containing Practical Hints and Original Recipes of Tasty Dishes for the Dinner and Supper Table, will be sent Post Free on receipt of Address, by ALFRED BIRD & SONS, Birmingham.

N.B.—Grocers can have Copies for Distribution among their Customers on Application.

A PROPOSAL For Every Lady.

TO MAKE DELICIOUS CUSTARDS WITH

BIRD'S CUSTARD POWDER

A DAILY LUXURY.

It Provides an Endless Variety of Dainty and Choice Dishes.

NO EGGS REQUIRED.

SOLD EVERYWHERE.

GUARANTEE of PURITY & EXCELLENCE

Every GENUINE PACKET bears the autograph signature of the Inventors and Sole Manufacturers—ALFRED BIRD & SONS.

ALWAYS INSIST UPON THIS.

In 1837 Alfred Bird invented this cornflour-based imitation custard powder because his wife was allergic to eggs. It remains popular, although some say it pales in comparison to authentic custard.

powders. Without mentioning a brand name, the 1898 edition of *The Encyclopædia of Practical Cookery: A Complete Dictionary of all Pertaining to the Art of Cookery and Table Service* reported that 'Blancmange powders are offered for sale in packets. They are made of some preparation of starch, and are pronounced good and inexpensive.'[23]

Germany's August Oetker found success by selling his baking powder, called Backin, to home cooks in small envelopes containing enough to leaven 500 g (1.1 lb) of flour. By 1906 the company had sold 50 million envelopes.[24] In America, the best-known brands included Rumford, Davis and Clabber Girl. Although controversy as to their safety arose, and some objected to their taste, by the turn of the twentieth century, cream of tartar, baking soda and baking powder were all being used in baking. The chemical leaveners saved time and, once they were considered safe and reliable, they sold well. Women's magazines printed recipes using the new products, and manufacturers promoted them in their own recipe books and brochures, often written by prominent cooks and cookbook authors.

Baking powder not only transformed desserts; it also inspired whimsical advertisements.

As early as 1895 the American Royal Baking Powder Company published a cookbook made up of recipes sent to the company by its customers. The book was titled *My 'Favorite Receipt'*, and included recipes for pies, cookies, puddings, doughnuts and cakes as well as savoury dishes and beverages. Naturally most, though not all, of the recipes called for Royal Baking Powder. One, for 'Election Cake (My Great Grandmother's)', sent in by Mrs Stephen Gilman of Lynnfield, Massachusetts, called for one teaspoon of Royal Baking Powder because 'doubtless Grandma would if she'd had it'.[25] Most of the recipes in the book were still written paragraph-style and did not specify details such as mixing procedures, pan sizes or temperatures. This one is typical:

TEA BISCUIT

1 qt. cream, 2 qts. flour, 4 teaspoons Royal Baking Powder,

1 teaspoon salt; bake in a quick oven from 10 to 15 minutes.

– Mrs. James S. Parker, Freehold, N. J.[26]

A PRIDE OF PUDDINGS

Puddings have a long and storied history. Some form of bread pudding was and is made everywhere from Egypt to England, Italy to India, and it dates back to at least the Middle Ages. Recipes are many and varied. Hannah Glasse's meagre little bread loaf, soaked in plain milk, tied up in a pudding cloth and boiled, exemplified the most frugal of puddings. The French *charlotte aux pommes*, apple charlotte, with its well-buttered layers of bread and apples, was among the richer and more indulgent.

Rice pudding was enjoyed in Asia for centuries before the West discovered it, and nearly every area in India has its own version. In south India it is called *payasam*, and the tiny state of Kerala boasts two *payasams*, one black and one white. Black ones are made with coconut milk, jackfruit preserves, bananas or rice, along with jaggery (an unrefined brown sugar). White ones are made with cow's milk, sugar, and rice or vermicelli. Kerala in southwest India is said to mean 'the land of coconut trees', and coconut is prominent in the area's desserts. According to Vrinda Varma, assistant professor at Sree Kerala Varma College, the 'king of *payasams* is *chakka pradhaman*', which is made with jackfruit jam, coconut milk, coconut cream, ginger, coconut slivers and ghee (clarified butter).[27] Cashew nuts and/or raisins are sometimes added, but the pudding, unlike most *payasams*, does not contain rice.

Rice puddings can be plain and simple or lush with cream and lavished with candied fruits, liqueurs and custard, as is the French pudding *riz à l'impératrice*. Latin Americans add tequila-soaked raisins to their *arroz con leche*. The Portuguese decorate their *arroz doce* with swirls of cinnamon on festive occasions. But when it is left plain and unadorned, rice pudding can be dull and boring. In A. A. Milne's poem 'Rice Pudding', yet another serving has Mary Jane 'crying with all her might and main'.[28] Rice pudding was a regular nursery meal in 1920s England when Milne wrote the poem, and he knew how tiresome it could become.

England's classic steamed puddings such as plum, suet, roly-poly and spotted dick originated as the meat and blood puddings of ancient Greece and were sausage-like mixtures packed into a cleaned animal intestine and boiled. They were made right after the animal was slaughtered as a means of using up all of the perishable meat, blood and offal. One of the most famous of these puddings is haggis, acclaimed by Robert Burns as the 'Great chieftain o' the pudding-race!' Clearly savoury rather than sweet, these puddings had the disadvantage of requiring intestines, so they could be made only at slaughtering time. During the seventeenth century, someone had the happy idea of using a densely woven cloth, instead of stomachs or intestines, to enclose the pudding mixture. The pudding cloth was hardly a technological wonder, but it began to transform puddings. Initially, they were still hearty meaty dishes, but gradually cooks began adding fruits, sugar and spices

Making the Christmas pudding was a family affair in 19th-century England.

and creating lighter, sweeter puddings: dessert puddings. The plum pudding Charles Dickens made memorable in *A Christmas Carol* was such a pudding. It is still Britain's essential Christmas dessert, whether homemade or shop-bought.

When manufacturers began mass production of tin pudding moulds in the nineteenth century, puddings became more popular than ever. By the nineteenth century, in England a meal was hardly a meal without a pudding. Eliza Acton had dozens of recipes in *Modern Cookery for Private Families*, from 'The Publisher's Pudding', which 'can scarcely be made *too rich*', to 'Poor Author's Pudding'. Even households without servants in the kitchen could produce lovely steamed, moulded puddings. In the U.S., Esther Allen Howland had fifty pudding recipes in her book *The New England Economical Housekeeper*. Puddings were also served in other lands and at the other end of the social spectrum. The famed French chef Urbain Dubois included a recipe for a moulded English plum pudding in his *Artistic Cookery: A Practical System for the Use of the Nobility and Gentry and for Public Entertainments*. He said plum pudding was known and served in all countries, but his version would produce the best results.[29]

This is a rather simpler pudding recipe from Mrs Beeton:

ALMA PUDDING.
1237. INGREDIENTS. – 1/2 lb. of fresh butter, 1/2 lb. of powdered sugar, 1/2 lb. of flour, 1/4 lb. of currants, 4 eggs.
Mode. – Beat the butter to a thick cream, strew in, by degrees, the sugar, and mix both these well together; then dredge the flour in gradually, add the currants, and moisten with the eggs, which should be well beaten. When all the ingredients are well stirred and mixed, butter a mould that will hold the mixture exactly, tie it down with a cloth, put the pudding into boiling water, and boil for 5 hours; when turned out, strew some powdered sugar over it, and serve.
Time. – 6 hours. *Average cost*, 1s. 6d.

Sufficient for 5 or 6 persons.
Seasonable at any time.[30]

JELLIES, EXCEPTIONAL AND EVERYDAY

The elegant jellies of the past had been so expensive and difficult to make that only the upper classes with servants to do all the work could serve them. Those who were lucky enough to have jellies revelled in them. Elizabethans flavoured theirs with ginger and cloves or rosewater and fresh strawberries. Robert May added colourings to his jellies and moulded them in scallop shells. Jellies arranged on tiered epergnes glistened in the candlelight of eighteenth-century tables. Finally, in the late nineteenth century, mass-marketed gelatines came onto the market and brought jellies within the reach of middle-class families.

Although more affordable and less time-consuming, some of the new products were not completely successful. Mrs Beeton said

With this two-part Wedgwood mould made at the turn of the 19th century, one poured clear jelly between the two moulds. After it had set, the plain outer mould was carefully removed, revealing the decorative mould through an outer layer of sparkling jelly.

The cacao plant depicted on an 1870 trade card.

they were 'never so delicate' as the gelatine made from calves' feet. An alternative was, according to the advertising, to purchase ready-made 'JELLIES of unequalled brilliance' from companies such as Crosse & Blackwell.[31] By the early twentieth century, however, reliable leaf gelatine and powdered, nearly instant gelatines in flavours from lime to blackcurrant had turned jellies into an inexpensive, quick and easy mainstream dessert. Manufacturers quickly produced recipe booklets to increase sales and, eventually, sold moulds to customers who sent them a small amount of money and several package fronts. Jellies became a commonplace, though much appreciated, dessert rather than an impressive centrepiece.

INTRODUCING CHOCOLATE

One of the most exciting and convenient new dessert ingredients was chocolate. Of course, there was nothing new about chocolate itself. The Aztecs and the Mayans had been drinking it for centuries. When the Spanish conquerors brought cacao beans to Europe in the sixteenth century, Europeans began drinking it, too. Happily for Catholics, drinking hot chocolate was allowed on fast days. It contained more fat than beverages such as coffee or tea so it was more filling as well as being tasty, which made it especially popular. In the late seventeenth century, it was drunk by fashionable citizens in London coffee houses and Paris cafés. But it was still a drink. Apothecaries and small dry goods shops sold coarsely ground, unsweetened cakes of chocolate, which could be grated or melted for use either as a drink or, less frequently, in a recipe. Latini made chocolate ice cream, and some confectioners made chocolate custards, creams and dragées. But little chocolate was used in baking. One of the first commercial chocolate factories in the U.S. was the seemingly aptly named Baker's Chocolate Company, established in 1765 by James Baker in Dorchester, Massachusetts. However, the company did not produce baking chocolate for many years. It produced tablets of drinking chocolate. Later, when the company did begin to manufacture baking chocolate, its name was an asset, and Baker's Chocolate became prominent in the business. Its ads were easily recognized for their image of a pretty serving maid, called *La Belle chocolatière*, based on a pastel by the Swiss artist Jean-Étienne Liotard.[32]

During the late nineteenth century, Dutch, Swiss and English chemists developed systems for processing cacao beans that completely transformed chocolate production and consumption. In Amsterdam, Coenraad Van Houten pioneered a method of grinding the beans that separated the cocoa butter from the cocoa mass and made a more homogenized, less oily powdered chocolate for drinking. In Bern, Switzerland, Rodolphe Lindt invented the process called 'conching', which results in smooth, clean, melting chocolate. In Bristol, England, Joseph Fry invented a hydraulic press

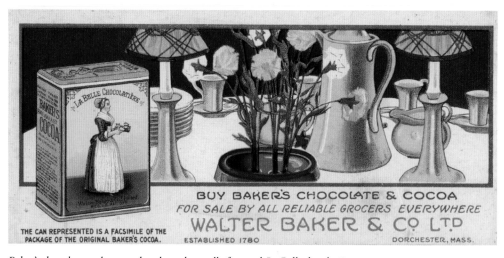

Baker's chocolate packages and trade cards usually featured *La Belle chocolatière*.

Chocolate, rather than molasses, swirls through a classic marble cake.

that produced chocolate paste that could be poured into moulds for bars.[33] The result of all this innovation was chocolate and cocoa products that were more convenient to use and more palatable than the early blocks of chocolate. And that meant more chocolate desserts.

Gradually, and then enthusiastically, home cooks and professionals everywhere began adding chocolate to their cakes, cookies, puddings, tarts, sauces and ice creams. Cookbooks featured new recipes and new interpretations of existing ones. Like other manufacturers, chocolate companies published cookbooks filled with recipes using their products, which were written by popular writers of the day. In the U.S., recipes using chocolate, often specifying a brand such as Baker's, flourished. Some desserts that are now typically made with chocolate were developed from ones that were originally flavoured and darkened with molasses. Today the swirling dark and light pattern of marble cake is made with vanilla and chocolate batters, but before the turn of the twentieth century, the darker part owed its colour to molasses and brown sugar, not chocolate. When chocolate became more accessible and fashionable, molasses came to be seen as an old-fashioned ingredient.

The chocolate dessert squares called 'brownies' were originally made with molasses. They are believed to have been named for a popular band of cartoon figures called the Brownies, which were created by the Canadian illustrator Palmer Cox in the 1880s. His merry sprites were featured in magazines, newspapers, songs, books and merchandise, including dolls, Christmas ornaments and children's cutlery. The Eastman Kodak Company's lightweight camera was also named for the Brownies. One of the earliest recipes for brownies using

Dessert brownies are among the many items named in tribute to Palmer Cox's cartoon characters.

chocolate rather than molasses came from a cookbook published by Lowney's, another Boston, Massachusetts, chocolate company. Lowney's Brownies became the most reprinted recipe in New England community cookbooks in the early twentieth century.

The first cartoon characters to be mass-merchandised, the merry sprites called 'Brownies' began in comic strips. As their popularity grew, they became everything from paper dolls to bowling pins.

LOWNEY'S BROWNIES

½ cup butter

2 eggs

1 cup sugar

½ cup nut meats

2 squares Lowney's Premium chocolate

½ cup flour

¼ teaspoon salt

Cream butter, add remaining ingredients, spread on buttered sheets, and bake ten to fifteen minutes. Cut in squares as soon as taken from oven.[34]

INSTANT SUCCESS

In the professional confectionery world during the late nineteenth century, confectioners were publishing pastry manuals using new printing techniques, such as colour graphics, to show creations off to their best advantage. Jules Gouffé's books, published in French and then in English, led the way. They were quickly followed by those of German confectioners such as Johannes Martin Erich Weber, who used colour illustrations in books that were translated into English, Spanish, Swedish and French.[35] *The Book of Cakes*, published in 1904 by the English confectioners T. Percy Lewis and A. G. Bromley, featured colourful cake designs that had won prizes at various exhibitions and competitions. The authors wrote that 'cake decoration is still very much in its infancy',[36] and illustrated basic frosting and piping techniques as well as complex designs. The book included recipes for a variety of cakes, from spectacularly decorated birthday, Christmas and christening cakes to simpler, more affordable cakes for bakers with less affluent customers. 'Penny School Cakes' and 'Shilling and Sixpenny Sponge Cakes' were part of the mix, along with marzipan gâteaux and three-tier wedding cake.

In addition to recipes and designs, professional confectioners had to consider mundane issues such as pricing, shop displays and shelf life. Trade journals and books included sales and display advice along with recipes, and they carried advertising for a plethora of products and equipment for bakers, pastry makers, ice-cream makers and other professionals. The books advertised essentials such as icing sugar, icing colours, gum-paste cake ornaments and fondant, as well as a variety of icing pastry bags and piping tips used to form leaves, stars or flowers. They also included the nails on which to form icing flowers before transferring them to the cake. There were advertisements for pre-made icing flowers and other decorations, gas pastry ovens, cake dummies (used for display purposes) and cake boxes.

Agnes Marshall was a successful nineteenth-century cook, lecturer, entrepreneur, London cooking school founder and author of books including *Mrs. A. B. Marshall's Cookery Book*, *The Book of Ices* and *Fancy Ices*. Her books revealed her business acumen by featuring ads for her many branded products, including extracts, ice-cream freezers, moulds, icing bags and tips for piping, gelatine, vegetable colours and even Marshall's pure cane sugar and icing sugar. She was also one of the first to serve ice cream in cones, although hers were served as elegant dinner party desserts rather than street food.

Frederick T. Vine, the English confectioner who was editor of the trade magazine the *British Baker* – and author of a series of books for the trade including *Ices: Plain and Decorated*; *Biscuits for Bakers: Easy to Make and Profitable to Sell*; *Practical Pastry: A Handbook for Pastrybakers, Cooks and Confectioners*; and *Saleable Shop Goods*

for Counter-tray and Window: (Including 'Popular Penny Cakes.')
A Practical Book for All in the Trade – wrote about the practical side
of the confectioner's work. Along with his recipes and illustrations,
he noted the prices shopkeepers could expect to get for the various
ices, cakes, biscuits and pastries. Vine suggested that those who were
located in affluent neighbourhoods might increase or even double the
suggested price. His books included ads for practical utensils geared
to the trade including stoves, ice-cream freezers, an almond slicer and
grinder, and more. Some of the advertising featured the instant or faux
products, like Bird's powdered blancmange, that would only grow more
common in the years to come. The 1907 edition of Vine's *Saleable Shop
Goods* included an advertisement for 'Regal Compound' that explained
that it was

> made of vegetable fat. It is sweet, pure, digestible, and neutral.
> From hygienic authority it is healthier, richer, and more whole-
> some than hog lard, while in price it represents a very great saving
> . . . useful for all the cheaper kinds of Biscuits, and for the better
> kinds used with butter . . . specially adapted for Cake-Making
> and Culinary purposes.[37]

To his credit, Vine advised against using such compounds in his dis-
cussion of ingredients. He wrote, 'to the veriest novice in the trade,
it must be at once apparent that butter for all kinds of confectionery
takes first place, and if your business is first-class, do not be deluded
into purchasing anything else.'[38] He also advised avoiding eggs with
pale and small yolks, as they would necessitate using egg colours to
make confections look as rich as they should. 'Egso, the natural egg
yellow', used 'by all the leading Cake and Biscuit Manufacturers at
Home and Abroad', was widely advertised to the trade, though clearly
Vine did not approve of it.

DOMESTIC SCIENTISTS

At the time, cookery schools were proliferating in Europe and the U.S. as a result of the new domestic science movement. Schools including Mrs Marshall's National Training School of Cookery, founded in London in 1883, introduced girls to precise food preparation and readied them for service in aristocratic homes. England's National Training School for Cookery was intended to produce teachers of cooking. Schools in Scandinavia and Germany for working-class women and farm wives also taught scientific approaches to cooking. Later, in Germany in the years after the First World War, the domestic science movement focused on the country's economic recovery rather than such advantages as increased leisure time or the use of new cooking implements. As the food historian Ursula Heinzelmann has pointed out, many regions of Germany were impoverished in the post-war years, and some families suffered terrible economic hardships. The efficiency of the scientific approach to cooking and home management was intended to ensure that they would not go hungry.

In the U.S., the most famous home economics or domestic science school was the Boston Cooking School, which was founded in 1879. The school's first principals were Mary J. Lincoln and later Fannie Farmer, both of whom wrote cookbooks in addition to teaching. The new home economists, as they came to be known, were exacting in their classes, as well as in the books and magazine articles they published. Their recipes brought new rigour to cooking. They stressed exact measurements, nutrition and digestion more than flavour and enjoyment. An unintended consequence of their influence was a method of cooking that relied on following instructions rather than judgement and a sense of taste.

Mass-produced implements proliferated during the Victorian era, and those who could afford to do so outfitted their kitchens with new, time-saving gadgets. Women's magazines and cookbooks not only advocated the use of easy-to-use products and equipment, but

The young girls in this 1893 photograph at an unidentified cooking school took their cooking lessons seriously.

often included lists of tools that the well-appointed kitchen should have. Over time, the lists grew longer. Mrs Beeton listed some, writing that more were to be seen in catalogues. Her list included a tea kettle, a toasting fork, a bread grater, skewers, a coffee pot, various pans, a flour box, jelly moulds and freezing pots for making ice cream.

Maria Parloa listed many more in *Miss Parloa's New Cook Book and Marketing Guide*, published in Boston in 1880. In her section on 'Kitchen Furnishing', she wrote, 'If there be much fancy cooking, there must be an ice cream freezer, jelly and charlotte russe moulds and many little pans and cutters.' She said one should get the essential items first, and then 'add those used in fancy cooking'. Her list of utensils a kitchen should be furnished with included a waffle iron, a Dover egg-beater, a variety of baking pans, two tin muffin pans, a chocolate pot, pudding moulds and dishes, a cake box, a spice box, dredgers for flour and for powdered sugar, mixing spoons, tablespoons, a jagging iron for cutting pastry decoratively, a biscuit cutter, an apple corer, a rolling pin, a whip churn for whipping cream, pie moulds, a ladyfingers pan, confectioners' tubes and more. Parloa, a cook, teacher of domestic science, cookbook writer and columnist for the *Ladies' Home Journal*, recommended some items by their manufacturer's brand names. Lest there be any doubt of her motives in endorsing products, she wrote that 'there is not a word of praise which is not merited, and that every line of commendation appears utterly without the solicitation, suggestion or *knowledge* of anybody likely to receive pecuniary benefit therefrom.'[39]

Before long, in the U.S., even those who lived far from shops other than a general store could equip their kitchens handsomely. Inexpensive postal rates helped make the mail order business feasible, and the railroad made the delivery of goods to rural communities a reality. Within a few years, mail order shopping became a convenience across the country. In 1888 Richard Sears, a railroad station agent in Minnesota, began selling watches through a printed mailer. Sears moved to Chicago and, along with his partner, Alvah Roebuck, produced catalogues selling everything from guns to women's shirtwaists, from sewing machines to kitchenware, at reasonable prices. The Sears catalogue of 1897 sold the latest stoves, waffle irons, jelly cake pans, tube cake pans, muffin pans, Turk's head pans, moulds for puddings and ice creams, tin measuring cups, Dover egg-beaters and much more. Homemakers in small western hamlets now had access to the same cooking supplies as their city cousins. As a result, they could enjoy the same desserts.

THE DESSERT MENU

As the world moved from the nineteenth to the twentieth century, many more dessert dishes were born. But restaurant menu writers had yet to agree on exactly how to label the dessert category. Although dessert had been a separate course of sweet dishes since the mid-nineteenth century, when *service à la russe* was introduced, it still went by many different names on restaurant, hotel and banquet menus. Some listed two different categories, some three; a few had more. If there were two, the first was generally 'Pastry' and consisted of various cakes, charlotte russe, ladyfingers, meringues, pies, tarts and puddings. The second was 'Dessert' and, as might be expected, consisted of fruits and nuts, just as it would have centuries before. But many menus also included ices, ice creams or gelatines under the dessert heading, along with fruit. Some American menus used the heading 'Puddings and Pastries', rather than simply 'Pastry'. Under their 'Dessert' heading, they listed ice creams, fruits and nuts.

The Astor House in New York had four headings on one of its mid-nineteenth-century menus: the first, 'Ornamental Pastry', listed 'Gothic Temple' and 'Nougat of Flowers'; the second, 'Pastry', included charlotte russe, Swiss meringues, champagne jelly, French cream cakes, Bavarian cheese, rum jelly and omelette soufflé; under 'Confectionary' were punch cakes, macaroons, kisses, almond cakes, ladyfingers and Boston cream cakes. The fourth and final one was simply 'Fruit'.[40]

A menu of 1886 from the Granville Hotel, England, written in French as so many menus were, had three categories. *Entremets* consisted of *tartes aux prunes, gelée au citron, compote de poires à la crème* and *tartelettes à la pithivière*. Two ices were listed under *Glaces*: *biscuits glacés* and *l'eau d'ananas*. The final heading, with nothing listed under it, was *Dessert*.[41]

Similarly, the menu for a dinner held by King Leopold II and Queen Marie-Henriette in Brussels on 26 May 1894 had three dessert headings: *Entremets de douceur*, consisting of *pudding soufflé à la Woronzoff* and charlotte russe; the *Glaces* were *vanille* and *cerise*; finally, there was *Fruits, Dessert*, which did not have anything listed beneath the heading. Presumably it consisted of various fruits and an assortment of nuts.[42]

Steamship
"North West"

LUNCHEON.

MONDAY, JULY 11, 1898.

SOUPS.

Cold Consommé, en tasse......20	Julienne......30	
Consommé......30	Tomato......30	
Consommé Solferino......30	Chicken Gumbo......30	

Broiled Whitefish, á la Maitre d'Hotel......50

SALADS.

Potatoes......20	Watercress......25	Chicken......65
Onions......30	Cucumbers......30	Lobster......70
Celery......25	Tomatoes......30	Macedoine......50
Lettuce......25	Cold Asparagus......35	Shrimp......50
	Salmon en Gelée......60	

COLD MEATS.

Roast Beef Sandwich.......20	Turkey......60	Westphalia Ham......60
Ham or Tongue "......15	Corned Beef......40	Paté de foi gras......70
Chicken "......20	Tongue......40	Boned Turkey......65
Sardines......30	Ham......40	Roast Quail......75
Roast Beef......50	Chicken......70	Roast Squab......75

VEGETABLES.

Boiled Potatoes......15	Boiled Rice......20	Peas......25
Potatoes, French Fried......15	Stewed Tomatoes......25	Onions in Cream......25
Mashed Potatoes......15	Butter Beans......25	Potatoes in Cream......25

ROASTS AND ENTREES.

Leg of Mutton, Caper sauce......55	Escallops of Veal, á la Milanaise......55
	Ribs of Beef, au Jus......50

CHEESE.

American......15	Fromage de Brie......25	Swiss......25
Edam......20	Roquefort......25	Club......25
	Neufchatel......20	

PASTRY AND DESSERT.

PRESERVES.

Pumpkin Pie......15	Preserved Apricots......25
Marmalade Tarts......20	" Green Gages......25
Vienna Ice Cream......25	" Strawberries......25
Vanilla Ice Cream......25	" Raspberries......25
Chocolate Ice Cream......25	Canton Ginger......30
Tutti Frutti Ice Cream......25	Raspberry Jam......25
Punch Muscovite......25	Strawberry Jam......25
Punch au Kirsch......25	Peach Jam......25
Punch Romaine......25	Pear Jam......25
Punch Marasquino......25	Gage Plum Jam......25
Punch au Kummel......25	Quince Jam......25
Punch Benedictine......25	Brandy Peaches......35
Assorted Cake......25	" Pears......35
Pound Cake......25	Cherries......35

Orange Marmalade......25	Red Raspberries......25
Honey......30	Peaches......25
Stewed Prunes......20	Watermelon......25
Oranges......20	Strawberries......25
Bananas......20	

Coffee, single pot......20	Tea, single pot......20
Coffee, large pot......30	Tea, large pot......30
	Milk, per glass......10

HOURS FOR MEALS:

Breakfast, 7 to 11.   Lunch, 12:30 to 3:30.   Dinner, 5:30 to 9:30.   Central Time.

Typically, this late 19th-century steamship menu used the heading 'Pastry and Dessert', rather than simply 'Dessert'.

It was not until the 1920s that 'Dessert' became the predominant heading on most menus with all the sweet dishes listed under it, from ice cream to sponge cake to fruit.

In homes at the time, at least at the finest tables, there was a similar split. Dessert was often divided between a course of pastries or a cake and, after that, often with the tablecloth removed, just as Alexis Soyer's Mr B. had preferred, a course of sweetmeats consisting of nuts and dried and fresh fruits.

A truly ancient fruit cake, from the reign of Egypt's Thutmose II, *c.* 1492–1473 BC.

FIVE

DEVELOPING DESSERTS

CAKES HAVE A LONG and far-flung lineage, although the light and lofty cakes on our dessert menus have little in common with their early ancestors. It was not until the nineteenth century that cooks were able to create the enormous array of cakes with which we are familiar today. When the Industrial Revolution introduced new tools, equipment and ingredients, hundreds of cakes entered the repertoire, adorned the dessert table and delighted diners.

The cheesecakes of ancient Greece and Rome were compact discs of cheese and honey rather than today's rich and creamy cheesecakes. Fruit cakes, which were first steamed rather than baked, evolved from plum puddings, which themselves originated as meat-rich porridges. In Italy, Siena's famed fruit cake called *panforte* dates back to at least the Middle Ages. Rich with nuts and candied fruits, the flat, dense fruit cake has become a tourist attraction as well as a local favourite. The word *panforte* means strong bread, and the cake has also been called *panpepato*, or peppered bread, since pepper was predominant among its many spices. In the sixteenth century such spiciness was thought to be strengthening for women after childbirth, so friends and family often gave fruit cakes to new mothers.[1] The long-lasting quality of fruit cakes is sometimes ridiculed today, but it was a great benefit in earlier times.

During the Middle Ages, northern Europeans enjoyed a variety of gingerbreads, also known as honey cakes, which were often spiced

with pepper, caraway and anise seeds (as well as ginger). They were
initially made in Christian monasteries and convents, later by bakers
in professional guilds and eventually by home bakers. Early gingerbreads were often baked in elaborately carved moulds, much like wafer
moulds, depicting religious figures or lords and ladies. They became
popular throughout Europe and, eventually, in the U.S. In France,
gingerbread is known as *pain d'épice*; in Germany, *Lebkuchen* (in Nurem-
berg) or *Pfefferkuchen* (in Pulsnitz); in Italy, *pane di zenzero*; and in
Spain, *pan de gengibre*.

Today, bakers and home cooks everywhere from Berlin to
Birmingham build elaborately decorated gingerbread houses at
Christmastime, to the delight of children. However, the cottage that
lured Hansel and Gretel in the German legend that inspired the
Grimm brothers' fairy tale was originally constructed from both bread
and cake. The windowpanes were made of sugar. In later versions
of the story, the cottage was made from gingerbread and decorated
with sweets.

A wooden gingerbread mould from England, 19th century, probably used
to make gingerbread for a shop or a fair.

Pepper and other spices make Swedish *mjuk pepparkaka* a particularly tasty gingerbread cake.

Gilding the lily, this San Gimignano pastry shop tops its panforte with a layer of marzipan.

Many of our modern cakes descended from sweetened yeast-leavened breads; for example, *Gugelhupf*, which was traditionally served at festive occasions like weddings, christenings and holidays. Initially they were baked in bowls, later in turban-shaped moulds. The German word *Gugel* is derived from the Latin word for hood or bonnet, and *hupf* means jump or hop. In late medieval Austria, the *Gugelhupf* was decorated to form a festive headdress, and a bride would wear one ornamented with flowers and gleaming with candles atop her head to begin the dancing at her wedding feast.[2] Over time, these breads became lighter, sweeter and more cake-like, although today *Gugelhupf* is eaten as a breakfast bread or a snack with coffee or tea, not as a dessert cake. *Gugelhupf* falls under the category the French call *Viennoiserie* – sweetened, yeast-raised delights such as brioches and croissants that occupy a space between bread and cake. They might be sold at a *boulangerie* or a *pâtisserie*, but despite their delectability, they are not served for dessert.

A collection of exuberantly decorated *Gugelhupf* moulds.

In the U.S., the cakes known as Bundt cakes were inspired by the *Gugelhupf*, which is called *Bundkuchen* in northern Germany. But Americans called them Bundt cakes simply because they were baked in Bundt pans, not because they were any particular type of cake. They were also known as Turk's head cakes, because the swirling, fluted shape of the pan was thought to look like a turban. Today's Bundt cake recipes range from chocolate chip to pumpkin, and they are definitely dessert cakes.

Italian sweet breads such as panettone (*panetón* in Peru, *pan dulce* in Argentina), *pan d'oro* and *colomba* are all part of the same tradition. They might be served with breakfast, as a snack or, unlike most *Viennoiserie*, as a dessert. They are also related to the French *baba au rhum* and the Neapolitan *baba*. The word *baba* is from the Slavic term for old woman or grandmother. The name was thought to have been used because the cake's shape resembled an old woman in skirts. The cake dates back to the Middle Ages; however, the *baba* was not soaked in its signature rum syrup until the nineteenth century, when it became even more popular in Naples than in Paris.[3] The French ring-shaped savarin is a later addition to the family. It was named after

Soaked in rum, topped with whipped cream, rum babas are irresistible.

the gastronomic writer Jean Anthelme Brillat-Savarin, who famously wrote, 'Tell me what you eat, and I will tell you what you are.' The savarin is also made from a *baba*-type dough and soaked in rum syrup. Contrarily, these yeast-raised delights are considered desserts.

At the end of the Italian Renaissance, in his *Opera* of 1570, Bartolomeo Scappi described whisking egg whites to make sponge cake. This was one of the – if not *the* – first mentions of using eggs rather than yeast to lift and lighten cakes. Similar recipes quickly followed. Marx Rumpolt's *Ein new Kochbuch*, published in 1581, included a recipe for biscuits made with egg whites. When *Le Pâtissier françois* (thought to have been written by La Varenne), was published in 1653, the transition was complete. The recipes include *biscuit de Piedmont*, much like today's ladyfingers, and *biscuit de Savoie*, made in a mould like a madeleine, all of which are light sponge-cake-like mixtures that evolved from Italian recipes.[4] All became easier to make and more popular centuries later when electric mixers were invented. Today in Britain, the word 'biscuit' generally means the small, sweet baked item Americans call a 'cookie', but when *Le Pâtissier françois* was written, a biscuit was a sponge cake. The madeleine, of course, is the small sponge cake that unleashed the flood of memories Marcel Proust so richly recalled in *Remembrance of Things Past* (1913). He described the madeleine as 'the little scallop shell of pastry, so richly sensual under its severe, religious folds'.[5]

INVENTING CAKES

During the nineteenth century, propelled by new ovens, ingredients and kitchen supplies, the popularity and variety of cakes soared. By the end of the century, both home cooks and professionals made almond, carrot, chocolate, coconut, layer, loaf, marble (made with chocolate), pound, sponge, spice and both angel's and devil's food cakes. Nearly every country, many communities and some cooks developed their own special cakes. In urban areas, cakes might be purchased from pastry shops or made at home. But in remote or isolated areas without shops nearby, home cooks had no choice but to bake their own, and skilled cake-baking became a mark of achievement. This was particularly true in Britain, America and the Scandinavian countries.

Young Scandinavian women were supposed to have mastered seven different cakes or cookies before they married.[6] In rural areas in Sweden, it was traditional to entertain friends with a 'cake table' serving fifteen to twenty different cakes. Prominent among them were the layered sponge cakes known as *lagkage*, *blødkage* and *tårta*. The cakes were made to suit the season. In summer, women spread the layers with custard and fresh berries; in winter, with jam or whipped cream. In Denmark, the simple pound cake called *sandkage* was known as 'every housewife's savior', because it was quickly made and stored so well it could be kept on hand for unexpected guests.[7]

Grapes are baked into this bundt cake for an extra burst of flavour.

Despite their historic differences, the Greeks and the Turks have in common the sugar-syrup-soaked semolina cakes called *revani*. Recipes differ slightly. The cakes may be flavoured with lemon or have ground almonds added to the batter. The syrup may be as simple as a mixture of sugar, water and lemon zest or it may be enhanced with cloves, cinnamon or brandy. Every cook has her own unique way of flavouring the cake. Part of the preparation is always the same, though. As soon as she takes the hot cake out of the oven, the cook pours the syrup over it, making the cake irresistibly sweet and moist. Practical cooks sometimes thriftily use the syrup left over from their spoon sweets for added flavour.

Fashionable nineteenth-century Russians followed French trends in their desserts, even leaving behind the Russian word *zayedki* in favour of the word *desert* [sic] after the French. But they borrowed one of their favourite cakes from the Germans. Called *Baumkuchen* (or tree torte), it was included in *A Gift to Young Housewives* by Elena Molokhovets, the cookbook that was considered a bible for middle- and upper-class Russian homemakers from its first edition in 1861 until the 1917 Revolution. According to the food historian Joyce Toomre, who translated and annotated the book in 1992, *Baumkuchen* were made in Germany and Austria beginning at the end of the seventeenth century, when recipes for sponge cake first became widespread. The cake's popularity spread throughout Europe and Russia, and it became a favourite for special occasions. No ordinary sponge cake, it was made by pouring cake batter over a rotating spit so that it cooked into conical layers. Toomre wrote that 'a slice of cake resembled the concentric rings of a tree stump'. When it was cooked and taken off the spit, a hole would be left in the cake's centre. It was customary to tuck a small bird such as a sparrow into the centre and close the opening with a bouquet of flowers. When the cake was served, the flowers would be removed and the bird would fly out and, quite probably, startle the guests – just as the blackbirds had flown out of Robert May's pie and into a nursery rhyme.[8]

The many-layered splendours of *Baumkuchen*, without birds and flowers.

German cooks made *Kuchen* and elaborately filled *Torten*, but the German cake with worldwide acclaim is the chocolate sponge, sour cherry, kirschwasser, whipped cream and chocolate shavings extravaganza called Black Forest cake. The name comes from the traditional black, white and red costume of the Black Forest region, according to the food historian Ursula Heinzelmann. The cake originated in nineteenth-century professional kitchens; by the 1950s it began to appear in popular cookbooks.[9]

In Denmark they say everyone has her or his own special recipe for *æblekage*, or apple cake. Some are made with cake batter topped with sliced apples, sugar and cinnamon, and baked. Others are no-bake apple cakes made somewhat like an English trifle by layering crushed macaroons, or buttered and browned breadcrumbs, with currant jelly and apple sauce, and then topping it all off with whipped cream. Whichever way *æblekage* is made, it is a homemade dessert. Danish pastry, also called *weinerbrød* or Vienna bread, is made by professional bakers.

The *opéra* is the sophisticated lady of French gateaux.

French pâtisseries are famed for their gateaux, many filled with rich pastry cream or chocolate mousse. Some are lavishly decorated; others, simple and sophisticated. One of the most minimally elegant is the *opéra*, an almond sponge cake soaked with coffee syrup, layered with chocolate ganache and coffee buttercream, and glazed with lustrous chocolate. Typically the word *opéra* is piped in script on its surface. Naturally, Parisians usually bought their gâteaux from one of the many pastry shops for which the city was famed. But French home cooks, especially those who lived in the country, baked desserts such as the pound cake *quatre quarts*, or four fourths. It is made with a pound each of just four ingredients – flour, eggs, sugar and butter – and traditionally baked in a loaf pan.[10] Pound cakes, typically made by mixing, or creaming, butter and sugar together to make them rise, are known for their moist texture and good keeping quality.

The earliest sponge cakes like Scappi's were made without butter or other fat, relying on beaten egg whites to achieve their lofty heights and airy texture. But over time butter, whole eggs and even baking powder became part of the sponge cake mixture. In the 1940s the aptly named Harry Baker created a sponge cake made with vegetable oil that came to be called 'chiffon cake'. After he sold the recipe to General Mills and it was published in *Betty Crocker's Picture Cook Book*, chiffon cakes became an American sensation.[11]

French haute cuisine was the topic of many cookbooks, but it was not until the nineteenth century that books about *cuisine bourgeoise*, or home cooking, began to be published. A prominent early one was Aglaé Adanson's *La Maison de campagne* (The Country House), published in 1822. Today, Adanson is famed for the garden she founded in 1805 at her property in Balaine, northwest of Moulins, which is still open to the public. Adanson's two-volume work includes information about managing a country estate, a treatise on the eight hundred plant varieties grown on the estate and, as the food historian Barbara Ketcham Wheaton wrote, 'an excellent, practical cookbook'. 'Her recipes are refreshingly original,' Wheaton continued, and they 'work well'.[12] This is Wheaton's translation of Adanson's recipe for a cake home cooks would make.

GÂTEAU À LA LANGUEDOCIENNE
A cake in the Languedoc manner

Take 250 grams of flour and 250 grams of grated sugar. Mix them with six egg yolks and 250 grams of melted unsalted butter. Beat this batter for fifteen minutes. Add to it the six stiffly-beaten egg whites. Butter a very shallow pie plate which is 12″ in diameter. Pour your mixture onto it and arrange some pieces of blanched almonds on it. Bake in the oven with a gentle heat for an hour.[13]

The desserts of countries along the Danube were internationally famous in the era preceding the First World War, from the vast

The ethereally light soufflés called *Salzburger Nockerl* are said to be a tribute to the area's snow-capped Alps.

Named for the city of Linz on the Danube, jam-filled *Linzertorte* is redolent of cinnamon, cloves and almonds or hazelnuts, and always features a decorative lattice top.

selection of fruit-filled strudels enfolded in tissue-thin pastry to the multi-peaked soufflé called *Salzburger Nockerl*. Like Parisians, Viennese women had little reason to bake at the time because there was a *Konditorei*, or pastry shop, on nearly every corner. If she had servants to see to the whipping of egg whites and grinding of nuts, the mistress of the house might oversee the making of a cake that rivalled a pastry chef's, but otherwise she would stroll to a shop and buy one of a dizzying array of cakes and other pastries. Or she might meet a friend at a pastry shop for *Jause*, the afternoon treat of coffee and torte, or cake, accompanied by the omnipresent clouds of whipped cream called *Schlagobers*. She might choose a *Linzertorte*, a butter-rich almond or hazelnut tart filled with raspberry or apricot jam. Or possibly a *Sachertorte*. Among Vienna's most famous and controversial cakes, the *Sachertorte* was created by Franz Sacher, a caterer who worked in

In Vienna, a city famed for its confections, the chocolate and apricot *Sachertorte* is a star.

Vienna in the mid-nineteenth century. After his death, the cake was the subject of a seven-year-long court case to decide whether the Hotel Sacher or Demel's pastry shop had the right to call its cake the 'genuine Sachertorte'. The Hotel Sacher won, and its version – a chocolate sponge cake covered in apricot preserves and glazed with chocolate – was deemed the official *Sachertorte*. However, the argument over the cake's origins and preparation continues, as does the baking and enjoyment of the cake.[14]

Chocolate and apricot are a wonderful pairing. An American cookbook by Celestine Eustis, *Cooking in Old Creole Days* (1903), included a recipe with the unappetizing name 'Leonie Penin's Dry Cake'. It was a chocolate variation of a simple pound cake, filled with apricot jam and topped with 'a nice chocolate icing'. Eustis's book celebrated the traditional foods of wealthy antebellum Southerners, and its recipes were credited to the black cooks of the South. Unfortunately, the book did not include any biographical information about Leonie Penin. Her cake was simpler than Sacher's, but as he did she knew how to combine flavours in an appealing way.

LEONIE PENIN'S DRY CAKE

One cupful sugar, one cupful flour, dried in the oven and sifted, one cupful butter, three eggs. Beat all together in a bowl very thoroughly. Butter two pie plates, and put a little flour in the plates, then put in your cake and bake in the oven.

The same receipt can be used for chocolate cake, putting all the dough in one pie plate, and when once it is cooked and cooled off, you slice in half and butter with apricot jam, and put the slices together again with a nice chocolate icing on top.[15]

Budapest's most celebrated cake is József Dobos's sophisticated *Dobos torte*, an impressive six-layer sponge cake, filled with chocolate buttercream and glazed with a glistening caramel topping. The caramel is cut into slices before it hardens and arranged on top to facilitate serving and also create an impressive appearance.[16] The city also became associated with the cake called *Rigó Jancsi*. Named for a renowned Gypsy violinist who infamously ran off with a then-married millionairess from America named Clara Ward, the cake is a chocolate lover's dream of chocolate sponge, chocolate cream filling and chocolate glaze.

Though better known for their many puddings, English cooks did have cake specialities, some of which continue to be made. However, they are more apt to be served at teatime than for an after-dinner dessert. The classic Madeira cake is a sponge cake flavoured with lemon, not Madeira. It was so named because it was often served accompanied by a glass of Madeira. The Victoria sandwich cake is an iconic English cake that has been made various ways over time. The Victorian-era *Book of Cakes* included a professional recipe for 'Cream Victorias', sponge cakes sandwiched together with a cream filling. They were glazed with apricot purée, decorated with chopped pistachios and sold by the slice. Mrs Beeton made 'Victoria Sandwiches' with jam or marmalade between the layers, hence the name 'sandwich' – the cake was then cut into rectangles that were stacked across each other. Today, a Victoria sandwich is usually a single-layer cake sliced in half, filled with jam and topped with a sprinkling of icing sugar. An American version is called Washington pie. A slightly more distant relation is the official Massachusetts state dessert, Boston cream pie. Another layered sponge cake, Boston cream pie is filled with pastry cream and topped with a chocolate glaze. These cakes were called pies because originally they were baked in the same type of tin used for pies, as was Leonie Penin's cake.

One uniquely American cake is the white, fluffy angel-food cake. Made with egg whites, sugar, flour and flavouring, its creation depended on the use of cream of tartar to stabilize the egg whites. Because recipes called for whipping a dozen egg whites into foamy peaks, the egg-beater or whisk was also key to making the cake. Several versions were made in the late nineteenth century, but it was

An individual Boston cream pie, a speciality of Boston's Parker House Hotel.

the detailed recipe published in Fannie Farmer's *Boston Cooking-School Cook Book* that made the cake a household name and favourite dessert.[17]

CAKES IN ASIA

In Japan, *mochi*, sweet rice cakes, often stuffed with azuki bean paste, are a typical part of New Year celebration and the cherry blossom season. Traditionally, however, most meals ended with pickled plums rather than a sweet dessert. When the Japanese in Nagasaki were introduced to Western-style cakes and other baked goods by the Portuguese in the late sixteenth century, they named them *nanban-gashi*, 'Southern Barbarian cuisine'. Despite the negative sound of the phrase, the Japanese took to them with enthusiasm and creativity. Today, they joke that they have a second stomach reserved for dessert. They even have a word for it: *betsubara*. According to the Japanese chef Yoshio Saito, 'It's a combination of *betsu* meaning other, and *hara* meaning belly, with the *h* changing to a *b*.'[18] With a second belly, there's always room for dessert.

Today's Japanese desserts are likely to be innovative versions of Western ones. Japanese sponge cakes are based on the Portuguese cakes called *pão de ló*, but the Japanese flavour them with green tea. Japanese confectioners, like so many others, have fun with the shapes and names of their creations. The popular 'Grilled Sea Bream' sold by Tokyo vendors is made from a sweet batter baked in a mould shaped like a fish.[19] It calls to mind Mrs Eales's 'Trout-cream'.

Everyday Chinese meals did not include desserts, but banquets and special occasions called for two desserts. One might be a custard tart rather like the Portuguese *pastéis de nata*, rice pudding or banana fritters. The second dessert would nearly always be a sweet soup, which might be made from lotus seeds, pine nuts or wood ear mushrooms with peaches and cherries. One of the most time-honoured Chinese sweets is the mooncake, which is eaten during the Mid-autumn Festival.

With their symbolic designs and rich fillings, mooncakes are traditional Chinese Mid-autumn Festival sweets.

Typically, it is a round pastry filled with red azuki bean paste, lotus seed paste or sweet black bean paste. A salty duck egg yolk might be baked into the centre to symbolize the full moon. The top of the cake is imprinted with the Chinese characters for longevity or the rabbit who is said to live on the moon. Mooncake fillings vary according to regions, and contemporary cooks sometimes fill the cakes with ice cream.[20]

NAMES AND PLACES

Cakes and other desserts are frequently named for the city or region of their origin. The Paris-Brest, the ring- (or wheel-) shaped cake made from choux pastry – as éclairs and cream puffs are – was named for the bicycle race between Paris and Brest. The groundnut-filled pastry called *mostaccioli romani* originated as a Roman speciality. Bath buns and Chelsea buns, more often served as teacakes than after-dinner desserts, are both associated with their English places of origin.

But names and recipes also travelled freely across geographic boundaries. The *Spanische Windtorte* is Austrian in origin. Italians call their sponge cake *pan di Spagna* and use it as the base for the cake called *zuppa inglese*; the French call their sponge cake *Génoise*. Their custard is crème anglaise. The well-known and seemingly American cake called baked Alaska marries ice cream and cake under an insulating layer of meringue and is often served aflame. The ultimate hot and cold dessert, it was reputed to have originated in the United States with the 1867 purchase of Alaska. But its ancestors included a dessert Chinese chefs had demonstrated to their counterparts in Paris a year earlier. It consisted of ice cream encased in pastry and baked. Shortly thereafter, French cooks made an ice cream and meringue dessert they called *omelette norvégienne*. Delmonico's, the premier nineteenth-century American restaurant, served a similar dessert and called it Alaska Florida. Fannie Farmer called it baked Alaska and that has been its name ever since. By any name, it never fails to surprise and delight guests.[21]

Cakes and other desserts were also named for famous people. The French Saint-Honoré pastry, a cake combining puff and choux

As their name suggests, *Kaiserschmarrn* are pancakes fit for an emperor.

pastries with a type of pastry cream lightened with egg whites, was named for the patron saint of bakers and pastry chefs. The pastry cream is called *crème chiboust* for its creator, M. Chiboust, a French pastry chef. *Schillerlocken*, crisp rings of pastry baked in the shape of tubes or horns and filled with whipped cream or meringue, were named for the golden ringlets of the German poet Friedrich Schiller.

The famed French chef Auguste Escoffier created *pêches Melba* for the Australian opera singer Dame Nellie Melba when he was chef at the Savoy Hotel in London. It is a relatively simple combination of vanilla ice cream, peaches and raspberry sauce. However, Escoffier served it in a style befitting a star. In tribute to her performance in the opera *Lohengrin*, he served the dessert in a swan carved from ice and swathed in spun sugar.

Australia's famed Lamingtons were named for Lord Lamington, who was Governor of Queensland from 1896 to 1901. They are small squares of sponge cake, glazed with chocolate and covered with grated coconut. The first printed recipe appeared in 1902 in the cookery section of the *Queenslander*, a weekly newspaper, and was credited to 'a subscriber'.[22] The cakes became a staple of home cooks' repertoires. Today, packaged versions are sold in supermarkets.

MANY, MANY MERINGUES

One of the most versatile items in the dessert chef's kitchen, meringues can be swirled over pies, piped into individual shells to hold scoops of ice cream or other fillings, flavoured in countless ways, baked to make small cookies or biscuits, poached and floated atop crème anglaise to make *île flottante*, or floating island, or combined with cream to make the most ethereal of desserts.

New Zealand's light and airy Pavlova cake, named for the ballerina Anna Pavlova, is one example. When Pavlova toured New Zealand in the early twentieth century, pastry chefs created a variety of desserts in her honour. The one that endured and became an international

Pavlova, the perfect picnic dessert.

favourite among home cooks and pastry chefs alike is a froth of a meringue cake, baked to a crisp exterior with a soft interior, and topped with whipped cream and fresh strawberries. New Zealanders make it their own by using kiwi fruit in place of the strawberries. It is as elegant as the ballerina herself.

The happy marriage of meringue and whipped cream is also exemplified in the impressive *Spanische Windtorte*. It consists of built-up rings of meringue which are baked and then filled with whipped cream flavoured with cognac or enhanced with strawberries, crushed macaroons or toasted hazelnuts. Joseph Wechsberg wrote that the cake could be prepared without decoration, but clearly he preferred a more ornate version. Wechsberg, a Czech musician, writer and fine-dining aficionado, wrote that the sides of the cake were to be '*geschnörkelt* (curlicued) in meringue rosebuds and seashells, decorated with crystallized violets', and topped with a 'curvy cornice', which was also made from rings of meringue. He called the cake 'a baroque triumph in conception, design and execution, besides tasting of heaven'.[23] Wechsberg wrote that Austrians called meringue 'Spanish wind' because they identified elegance with Spain. However, the food historian Michael Krondl believes the name comes from a contemporary German word for morning glory, *Spanische Winde*, rather than the country of Spain.[24]

Another happy meringue and whipped cream pairing, but at the opposite end of the elegance spectrum, is the English dessert Eton mess. Named for the boys' school, it is a mishmash of broken pieces of meringue, whipped cream and strawberries. It looks like what might happen if a mischievous little boy broke into a *Spanische Windtorte* or a Pavlova before the party. Nevertheless, it tastes as delectable as the others and is a good deal easier to prepare.

Yet another light, frothy meringue and cream confection is the Blitz cake, also known as Blitz Torte. Its unusual feature is that the meringue layer is baked atop the cake batter. This is a family recipe from Roz Cummins, a Boston, Massachusetts-area writer.

ROZ'S BLITZ CAKE
Cake Layer
½ cup (120 g) butter
½ cup (100 g) granulated sugar
¼ teaspoon salt
4 egg yolks
1 teaspoon vanilla

3 tablespoons milk

1 cup (120 g) plain (all-purpose) flour

1 teaspoon baking powder

Meringue Layer

4 egg whites

¾ cup (150 g) granulated sugar

½ teaspoon ground cinnamon

½ cup (110 g) sliced blanched almonds

Whipped Cream

1 cup (240 ml) whipping cream

2 tablespoons sugar

Berries

2 cups (300 g) strawberries (or blueberries, raspberries, blackberries)

2 tablespoons sugar

Preheat oven to 175°C (350°F). Grease and flour two round 8- or 9-inch cake pans.

Cream the butter with sugar and salt, then beat in egg yolks, vanilla and milk. Stir in flour and baking powder. Beat until they are well incorporated, and the batter is smooth. Spread mixture in cake pans.

In another bowl, beat egg whites with sugar and the cinnamon until stiff. Spread meringue over the batter in each pan. It's hard to do this evenly. Don't worry too much about it. Top with almonds.

Bake the cake layers for 30 minutes (or about 25 if you use the bigger pans) or until cake just begins to pull away from sides of pan. Remove from oven, cool slightly, and remove cakes from pans to cool completely on a wire rack. While the cakes are cooling, make the whipped cream by adding the sugar to the chilled cream and whip.

Slice the strawberries into a bowl and toss them with the sugar. Do this about 20 minutes before serving. Place cake layer on a serving plate, meringue side up. Just before serving, scatter some strawberries on the bottom layer, spread with half of the whipped cream. Place the second layer on top, meringue side up. Top with the rest of the strawberries and whipped cream. Serve to the delight of eight to ten people. Best made the day of serving.

A Pastry Chef and his Cakes

Home cooks, in general, made relatively simple cakes for dessert. Confectioners, on the other hand, competed to make the most fanciful, elaborately decorated cakes. During the Victorian era, for professionals, creating elaborate desserts was a competitive sport, a way to demonstrate one's skill and imagination. The French-born English chef Alexis Soyer was a champion.

Soyer wrote that *pièces montées* were passé and said,

> I know many epicures that would object to sit down before those once favourite monuments, or colossal sugar ornaments, the modern table embellishments having very properly fallen into the hands of the silversmith. Simplicity, the mother of elegance, being now the order of the day.[25]

But there was nothing simple about the desserts Soyer produced, nor about the man himself. He was born into poverty and although his professional success meant that he hobnobbed with the rich and famous, he worked hard throughout his career to help the poor and hungry. Born in France in 1809, he began cooking at a young age. When he was 21, he moved to England, and within a few years was a celebrated chef. Ever the entrepreneur, he promoted his cookbooks, sauces and the kitchen appliances he designed and sold with flair. But Soyer also donated part of the profit from one of his cookbooks to the feeding of the poor. In 1847, during the Irish potato famine, he ran a soup kitchen in Dublin. He also travelled to Crimea during the Crimean War and worked with Florence Nightingale to improve the quality of the soldiers' food.

Soyer created cakes that rivalled the old subtleties or *pièces montées* for the members of London's elite Reform Club. In Soyer's hands, the fire-breathing boar's head that in medieval times was an actual boar's head became a cake shaped to look like one. He called it *Hure de sanglier glacé en surprise*, or mock boar's head. To make it, he carved a sponge cake into the shape of a boar's head, hollowed it out and filled it with lemon ice cream flavoured with curaçao. He frosted the cake with chocolate icing 'as near as possible to the colour of the real boar's head'. Soyer made the eyes from white icing and used cherries in the centres. He made the eyelashes from pistachio slivers; the tusks, from gum paste or *pâte d'office*. He glazed the boar's head with currant jelly, decorated it with croutons and served it on a silver platter.[26]

Again, as if reproducing medieval subtleties in sponge cake form, he made a peacock cake. He frosted his *Peacock à la Louis Quatorze* a 'pinkish white' and filled it with strawberry ice. The 'skins of some cherries' decorated the tail. He wrote, 'Any one perfect in sugar will form the tail open, which will produce a magnificent effect.'[27] As Soyer wrote, simplicity was the order of the day.

THE ICING ON THE CAKE

Decorating cakes with flair was easier after commercial refineries began producing confectioner's sugar, also known as icing or powdered sugar, in the nineteenth century. Earlier cooks had to crush sugar in a mortar, and then sieve it through a fine fabric such as silk to make it as smooth as possible before using it to ice cakes. Seventeenth-century cakes were often frosted with a simple syrup made by boiling sugar and water together and pouring the mixture over the cake. Then the cake was

Beautifully decorated gingerbread for Advent.

returned to the oven briefly so that the icing would harden into a glaze. The recipe titled 'To make an extraordinary good Cake' in Robert May's *The Accomplisht Cook; or, The Art and Mystery of Cookery* (1685) concluded by instructing the cook to boil sugar and water to 'candy height with a little rose-water, then draw the cake, run it all over, and set it into the oven till it be candied'.[28] Candy height was one of the stages of sugar boiling, akin to Massialot's *cassé*, or crack stage.

An alternative was to pile meringue atop a cake as soon as it was taken from the oven. Some cooks put cakes spread with meringue back into the oven to brown, but Amelia Simmons said 'it injures and yellows it, if the frosting be put on immediately it does best without being returned into the oven.'[29] Cooks also spread marzipan or fondant over cakes for a smooth and elegant finish.

By the nineteenth century, confectioners had created royal icing, a mixture of confectioner's sugar and beaten egg whites. It remains a cake-decorating mainstay. It can be spread smoothly over a cake and, more importantly, used to pipe decorative designs. Confectioners fell in love with the process, piping lacy designs, scrolls, names and

An illustration in Mrs Marshall's 1894 *Fancy Ices* demonstrates a rather precarious way to spin sugar to decorate ices.

messages such as 'Happy Birthday' or 'Good Luck' onto their cakes. They piped tennis racquets onto picnic cakes and cradles onto christening cakes. Multi-tiered wedding cakes became rococo celebrations of swirls, swags, lace and flowers. The term 'royal icing' was introduced when the frosting was used on Queen Victoria's wedding cake.

In *Mrs A. B. Marshall's Cookery Book*, published in 1888, Agnes Marshall wrote about a frosting she called 'Vienna icing'. She made it with icing sugar, butter and both rum and maraschino liqueur. Today, a similar version is called buttercream frosting or simply buttercream in English, or *crème au beurre* in French. Generally made with a flavouring such as vanilla extract, rather than the liqueurs she used, and often cream or milk as well as butter, it is the most common frosting used by home cooks.[30]

VIENNA ICING
Ten ounces of icing sugar and a quarter of a pound of butter worked till smooth with a wooden spoon; mix with one small wineglass of mixed Silver Rays (white) rum and maraschino, work it till like cream, then use. This may be flavoured and coloured according to taste.[31]

BISCUIT, *KOEKJE*, LITTLE CAKE, COOKIE

Biscuits are not complex confections. But they are difficult to define. The word comes from the Latin *panis biscoctus*, or twice-baked bread. Originally, biscuits were baked twice to cook out moisture and allow for long-term storage. Also known as rusks, ship's biscuits, *biscotti* and *zwieback*, these were all plain, dry biscuits that could go to sea or war or simply be stored in the pantry for months without becoming mouldy. Eventually they were sweetened and the term came to be used for a wide variety of items, many of which were neither twice cooked, nor plain, nor dry. *The Encyclopædia of Practical Cookery: A Complete Dictionary of all Pertaining to the Art of Cookery and*

One of the many colourful pre-Second World War English biscuit tins.

Table Service, published in London in 1898, and popularly known as *Garrett's*, for the name of its editor, T. Francis Garrett, was unable to define 'biscuit' clearly. It stated,

> Biscuit is universally adopted now by all Continental confectioners as applying in the broader sense to an extensive description of pastry goods which have only one apparent characteristic running throughout them, that of being baked brittle or crisp. Pastry-cooks and confectioners, both British and foreign, appear to have mutually agreed to retain this feature as the only one necessary to distinguish a tribe of kinds which differ from each other in almost every other particular. So greatly, indeed, do they differ, that it is almost impossible to attempt their classification, passing as they

do with rapid strides from dry to sweet, hard to soft, flaky to short, and plain to fancy, or from one combination to another.

The *Encyclopædia's* lengthy article included eight pages of biscuit recipes, along with illustrations of tools used in biscuit making, such as cutters and piping bags, as well as images of biscuit boxes and tins for storing biscuits. The recipes ranged from Abernethy biscuits, flavoured with caraway seeds, to York biscuits, cut into diamond shapes and baked in a 'sharp oven'. The book's 'Champagne Biscuits' were 'so called because they are very nice served with that wine'.[32] By the time it was published, the English were spelling the word as 'biscuit' rather than the earlier 'bisket', much to the dismay of the editors of the *Oxford English Dictionary*, who harrumphed that 'the regular form in English from the 16th to 18th cents. was *bisket*, as still pronounced; the current *biscuit* is a senseless adoption of the modern French spelling, without the French pronunciation'.

To add to the confusion, Americans in New Amsterdam transformed the Dutch word *koekje*, or little cake, to cookie. Amelia Simmons is credited with the first use of the word in a cookbook in her *American Cookery* (1796), and the usage spread. In the U.S. today, English biscuits are called cookies, and the word 'biscuit' is used for what the English would call a bun, muffin, or even a scone.

During the Victorian era, English manufacturers, many of whom are still in business, pioneered the mass production of biscuits. Although Anastasia Edwards, an English food historian, compared today's ubiquitous factory-produced biscuits to commodities such as toothpaste, she pointed out that eating them still evokes nostalgia among the British.[33] As if to prove her point, a couple who write under the joint pen name 'Nicey and Wifey' wrote a book about the pleasures of tea and shop-bought biscuits, called *Nicey and Wifey's Nice Cup of Tea and a Sit Down* (2004). Unapologetic about their preference for factory-made biscuits, they call digestives 'the undisputed king of the large-diameter biscuits . . . an iconic biscuit'.[34]

Americans, on the other hand, idealized home-baked cookies and filled the pages of cookbooks, magazines and the women's section of newspapers with recipes. Along with 'cookies', they were called nuts, kisses, snaps, crusts, cakes, stars, sticks, patties, drop cakes, rocks, shavings, hermits, jumbles, wafers and macaroons. Some were thin and crisp, as *Garrett's* definition stated, but others were soft and cake-like. The *Settlement Cookbook* (1904) had recipes for more than three dozen cookies, from almond to *pfefferneuesse*, from *springerle* to 'delicate zwieback'. Other cookbooks of the era were also rich with cookie recipes. Of course, buying cookbooks does not necessarily mean baking the recipes. Like the British, Americans also buy their share of commercially produced cookies and can be just as nostalgic about favourites, such as Oreos.

Some biscuits were and are elegant enough to grace the dessert table, especially when they accompany ice creams, sorbets, fruit compotes or custards. The jumble or knot, a seventeenth-century biscuit flavoured with rosewater or anise seed, was often depicted in still-life paintings along with the final course of comfits and wafers. Ladyfingers, also known as French Savoy biscuits, were served in the dessert course and also formed the basis of the popular charlotte russe. Other dessert-worthy biscuits include tuiles, the delicate biscuits shaped like rounded roof tiles; macarons, the colourful little almond biscuits, now often joined in pairs with a sweet filling, that originated in Renaissance Italy; and the small meringues called 'kisses' in English, and 'sighs' or *suspiros* in Spanish. The classic twice-baked biscuits *biscotti* – now sweetened and flavoured with almonds or other nuts, candied peel or seeds – are another dessert biscuit. Traditionally Italians, and today many others, serve them accompanied with a sweet wine such as Vin Santo at the close of many meals.

AS EASY AS (EATING) PIE

APPLE-PYE
Of all the delicates which Britons try,
To please the palate, or delight the eye;
Of all the several kinds of sumptuous fare;
There's none that can with Apple-pye compare,
For costly flavour, or substantial paste,
For outward beauty, or for inward taste.
When first this infant-dish in fashion came,
Th' ingredients were but coarse, and rude the frame;
As yet unpolish'd in the modern arts,
Our fathers eat Brown-bread instead of Tarts;
Pyes were but indigested lumps of dough,
Till time and just expense improv'd them so.
– William King (1663–1712)[35]

Before the turn of the eighteenth century, when the English writer William King wrote the poem excerpted above, the blackbirds had flown and standing pies filled with meats had been joined by more delicate pies and tarts with fruit or custard fillings. Fresh fruit tarts were made in season, and fruits were preserved to make wintertime tarts. In spring and summer, custard tarts were made with flowers such as primroses or marigolds. Almond tarts were flavoured with rose-water. Rhubarb, formerly used medicinally, began its long reign as a pie fruit (though it is classified as a vegetable). Apple pies were a traditional English favourite. They had been made since the Middle Ages, albeit then, as King suggested, in sturdy coffins rather than flaky pie-crusts. Such sweet pies might have been served at any time during the meal back then. Today they are strictly designated as desserts.

Mrs Glasse included several fruit and custard pies in the 1796 edition of *The Art of Cookery*. She had nine recipes for pie pastes or crusts, including a puff paste and a standing paste for great pies, which

Homey, old-fashioned apple pie never goes out of favour.

she said was 'fit for the walls of a goose pie'. Her 'crackling crust' was intended as a garnish for pies rather than a crust. It was made with pounded almonds and orange-flower water. Mrs Glasse's apple pie was made with a 'good puff-paste crust'. She directed the cook to make a syrup from apple peel, cores, mace, sugar and water. She said it was to be strained and cooked down 'till there is but very little and good', and then poured over the apples in the pie. Finally, the top crust was put on and the pie baked.[36]

The difference between a pie and a tart is not always clear. In general, pies have both a top and a bottom crust while a tart is usually made without a top crust. But exceptions are the rule. In England, fruit pies such as apple or plum are usually made in deep pie plates and have only a top crust. Fruit tarts are usually made in shallow pans, as are lemon curd and custard tarts. They are made with a bottom, but no top crust. However, the words 'pie' and 'tart' were and are often used interchangeably in English. Recipes for tarts often indicated a top as well as a bottom crust; pie recipes sometimes had only a bottom crust. A rhubarb pie in an American recipe of 1856 called for the cooked and sweetened fruit to be arranged on a pie plate without a bottom crust, and then covered with a top crust and baked.[37] The French tarte Tatin is baked with a top crust, and then turned over so that the crust is on the bottom, with the caramelized apples on the top. Small individual tarts are sometimes called 'tartlets', but the usage is inconsistent.

Mincemeat pie, although considered a dessert, contained meat in 1869 when this advertisement was created.

Europeans made an assortment of both pies and tarts, but nowhere were they more popular than in the U.S. Americans loved all sorts of pie, particularly sweet ones. They even ate pies for breakfast. Thanksgiving dinner always concludes with pie. It can be pumpkin, apple, cranberry, mincemeat, pecan or sweet potato, but it must be pie – not cake, not a soufflé, not ice cream, unless it's atop a slice of pie.

The popular American idiom 'as easy as pie' is thought to have originally been 'as easy as eating pie', partly because Americans ate so many pies and partly because it is easier to eat a pie than to bake one.

Perhaps because sweet dessert pies were so popular, some nineteenth-century American cookery writers did not approve of them. Mary J. Lincoln, of Boston Cooking School fame, called the apple the 'queen of all fruits', and recommended eating it in its natural state rather than making it into 'the persistent pie'.[38] Mrs Mary V. Terhune, who wrote under the pen name Marion Harland, was even more emphatic. She wrote that pie was a 'destructive sweet', called it indigestible and approvingly quoted a newspaper editorial that had called 'the weakness for pie . . . a national vice'.[39] Both of the women were popular writers, but they could not sway the public from its love of pies.

Later, in an editorial in the Saturday 3 May 1902 edition of the *New York Times*, an unnamed writer extolled the pie. He called it the 'American synonym of prosperity . . . Pie is the food of the heroic. No pie-eating people can ever be permanently vanquished.' The writer believed that the English had turned away from pie and that this was to their detriment. He wrote,

> It is a significant historical fact that England's glory was greatest in the days when her gallant sons ate pie . . . Then slowly the pernicious influence of the shopkeeping element grew, and gradually the generous dimensions of the pie were reduced, until now it has dwindled to the insignificant tart. As the pie declined the high ideals were lowered and the prestige and power of Great Britain dissipated.

Calling pie the 'calendar of the changing seasons', the writer went on to describe the perfect pie for each season of the year. He

Women learn how to bake pies, using Armour mincemeat, in this 19th-century advertisement for the American meatpacking company founded in Chicago.

began with apple, calling it the year-round pie. During the winter months, he wrote, the appropriate pie was mince, 'this highly spiced, juicy, and meaty composition having the power to maintain the normal temperature of the body in zero weather'. In spring he recommended 'the light and joyous custard, lemon, and rhubarb pies to quiet the tender yearnings for the undefined'. 'Lip-painting berry pies' and peach were pies for summer months. Finally, in autumn, 'as nature paints the forest with her magic brush, comes in the golden glory of the year, the royal pumpkin pie!'[40]

TABLE JEWELLERY

The plethora of cakes, pies and other desserts on turn-of-the-twentieth-century dessert tables presented a challenge for hosts and hostesses: which of the many pieces of newly available silverware should be used to serve them? A vast array of silverware was being produced at the time and, especially in the U.S., those who aspired to ascend higher on the social ladder were anxious to make the proper selection. The Russian style of serving courses in succession had led to the development of specific tableware for specific foods. As a result, a multitude of cutlery was available. At some tables cutlery was set out for each course and then replaced; at others, it was all laid out at the same time. The resulting array of silverware at each place led to much confusion and concern for newly affluent diners.[41] Now that there was a fork for every dish, 'Which fork should I use?' was a question wary diners frequently asked etiquette writers. The answer, generally, was whichever one your hostess was using. That must have made many guests pause to cast a surreptitious eye down the length of the table towards the hostess before tasting anything. A hostess had to learn not only which fork was appropriate, but which serving pieces were correct. Should she use asparagus tongs or asparagus servers, and which was the pudding spoon and which the blancmange? Fine dining and entertaining became fraught occasions ripe for faux pas for the inexperienced.

The proliferation of silverware was the result of several influences. The exploitation of silver mines in the American West after the Civil War cut the cost of silver dramatically and made it newly affordable. At the same time, the invention of electroplating brought relatively inexpensive silver plate to the table, and new die-stamping processes made elaborate ornamentation possible. Not only could the new flatware be decorated with monograms and family crests, but it could be adorned with nature motifs such as birds and flowers. These factors, coupled with post-Civil War prosperity in America, meant that families who had not dreamed of owning silver services, much less inheriting such things, could now afford them. They simply needed to learn how to use them.

Fortunate newlyweds in the U.S. could expect to receive silver tableware as wedding presents, according to William C. Conant, writing in the December 1874 issue of *Scribner's Monthly.* He said,

> so universal has the custom of bridal gifts become, hardly any
> comfortable young couple now begin housekeeping without
> a fair show of genuine table silver, as far at least as spoons, forks,
> butter, fruit, pie and fish-knives, napkin-rings, and such trifles.[42]

Of course, such silverware was still out of reach for many. But for those who could afford it, there was much to choose from. Forks, considered effete or ungodly in centuries past, now multiplied. They included forks designed specifically for salad, meat, fish, cherries, sardines, olives and oysters. The number of knives increased at the same rate. Butter knives, dinner knives, fish knives, fruit, dessert and cake knives were all available.[43]

One soup spoon was not enough. One needed small soup spoons for bouillon, larger ones for cream soups. There were spoons specifically for coffee, tea and chocolate, as well as tea caddy spoons, cream ladles, berry spoons, blancmange spoons, sugar spoons and more. The Towle Company offered customers nineteen different types

SYLVIA
HER MAJESTY
MARQUISE

"HOW WELL SHE ENTERTAINS!" . . . Such lovely silverware
in use at her party. And you can be just as charming a hostess. . . .
Here are three beautiful patterns from which to choose. Each has charm
and individuality and each is 1847 Rogers Bros. . . . the silverplate that
has graced the first tables of America since the year 1847. Yet, happily,
this finest of silverplate is most modestly priced. Six tea spoons—$3.25.
Remember, today's hostess has her "guest" set of silverware, just as
she has her "best" linen, china, and glass. Write Ann Adams, Dept. Z23,
International Silver Co., Meriden, Conn., for Buffet Party Booklet.

***IS** *This quality mark of the International Silver Company appears on every piece.*

1847 ROGERS BROS.
ORIGINAL ROGERS SILVERPLATE

Successful hostesses chose Rogers Bros. silverplate for guests.

of individual spoons and seventeen different serving spoons in its 'Georgian' pattern. The service was comprised of 131 pieces; a complete service for twelve numbered 1,888 pieces in all.[44]

Ice cream alone warranted a whole set of serving implements, including slicers, ornate hatchets and knives. One could eat ice cream using a spoon with a blunt end like a shovel, a spoon with a pronged end like a fork or an ice-cream fork. Ice-cream scoops were invented at the close of the century, but in general they were used by professionals rather than in the home.

In his article, which was titled 'The Silver Age', Conant described the splendours of one dining table in meticulous detail. When he reached the dessert course, he wrote,

> The ice-cream towers on massive silver stands sculptured with more Arctic scenery, to keep it from melting, with broad mirror trays beneath, the bountiful knife-edged ice-cream spoon, and the cool frost-finished saucers. There are also large vessels in kindred styles of art for fruit ices, with plates to match. The cakes and bon-bons are on low compotiers, or ornamented plates with stem and base, and the silver cake-knife has a fine saw back to its splendid blade, to divide the frosting without fracture.[45]

This sugar sifter spoon of *c.* 1855 was the stylish way to sprinkle sugar over one's fruit or pudding at the table.

He went on to describe the fruit bowl as a 'sort of fairy barge' containing the 'large yellow fruit from Havana and from Northern orchards', calling the arrangement 'apples of gold in pictures of silver'. He also noted the

> dainty *bijouterie* in silver and gold for sipping strong coffee, with the elegance of the dessert patterns in spoons, knives and nut-picks, and the silver knick-knacks for the passing around, lighting, and even ash-receiving of cigars.[46]

Of course, despite Conant's sweeping generalization, not every table was resplendent with silver or frosty moulded ice-cream towers. But in the final years of the nineteenth century, in most countries, dinners – whether in a simple home, in a grand mansion or in a restaurant or hotel – could conclude with a dessert. It might be cake, ice cream, pudding, pie or a simple serving of biscuits and fruit. Not limited to special occasions, dessert had become the natural ending for anything from a family supper to a formal banquet.

SIX

THE CONSTANCY OF CHANGE

AT THE TURN OF THE twentieth century, a new freedom swept through society high and low, as Victorian formality gave way to Edwardian ease and speed. Trains, steamships and automobiles were moving ever faster, and dining style was keeping pace. Artists, architects and designers were forging a new style and transforming houses, furniture, silverware and clothing. The creations of architects such as Walter Gropius, Ludwig Mies van der Rohe and Le Corbusier were not limited to the structures they conceived; they also influenced the way people lived in them, or aspired to. Elaborate table settings, ornate silverware and multi-course meals were anachronisms in a Bauhaus dining area.

Even among those who could still afford it, the ostentation of the 'Silver Age', as *Scribner's Monthly* had called it, came to be seen as excessive. In 1925 Herbert Hoover, then American secretary of commerce, recommended, and the Sterling Silverware Manufacturers Association adopted, a list of 55 items as the greatest number of separate pieces that should be in any new pattern.[1] By then many households had already begun to adapt to the new style. Immediately after the Great War, wrote one authority on social usage, 'formality was pushed aside with a great shout'.[2]

In addition to the war itself, women's suffrage, Hollywood, the Jazz Age and Prohibition were all blamed for or credited with the relaxing of standards. The historian Arthur M. Schlesinger wrote that in America the old rigid rules had been sustained by growing wealth and the aristocratic practices of the Old World, which the New World emulated. Not everyone followed the practices, he explained in his study of the changes, *Learning How to Behave: A Historical Study of American Etiquette Books*, but most were aware of them. Schlesinger believed that Prohibition, 'operating on the forbidden fruit principle, spread the habit of drinking in unexpected directions'; the automobile, which 'encouraged a more informal companionship of the sexes'; and the radio, which acquainted 'the remotest rural outposts with the changing urban ways and ideas', all helped spread new social values.[3]

In England, the complicated rules of etiquette and dining that were followed before the Great War were increasingly considered old-fashioned and outmoded. Enduring stiffly formal, multi-course dinners was seen by many, including the Prince of Wales, as a waste

Today, just as in the Middle Ages, wafers and wine are a perfect conclusion to dinner.

of time, as well as boring. In a biography written by a member of the royal staff, the prince (who became King Edward VII) was credited with launching the fashion for shorter dinners. He was not alone in wanting to dine in a faster, more contemporary fashion.[4]

For many others, the old style was no longer sustainable. During the war, tragically, some of the owners of grand English country estates had lost their sons and heirs. In addition, they lost the army of servants that had run the households, either owing to the war or because the men and women who would have gone into service in earlier times preferred employment in offices and factories. With neither sons to manage the estates nor servants to run them, many had to live simpler lives.

Lady Agnes Jekyll was an exemplar of her class and era. A Scottish aristocrat and renowned hostess, she was made Dame Commander of the British Empire for her work during the First World War. Later, she wrote a series of columns about food and entertaining, which were collected and published in 1922 as *Kitchen Essays*. Reflecting the times with wit and imagination, she wrote about coping with fewer servants and less money and embracing new ways of managing – she was also not too grand to serve guests American cereal as part of one dessert:

APRICOT PURÉE (WITH PUFFED RICE)
Stew 1 pound best dried apricots after an all-night soak. When cooked soft, add a small tin of peeled apricots; boil together, sweeten to taste; reduce the syrup, pass through a wire sieve, and put into a shallow glass bowl; cover completely with a thin layer of partly whipped cream (about 6d worth), and perhaps a few chopped pistachio nuts to embellish. With this send round a glass finger-bowl of that useful American cereal 'puffed rice' just crisped in the oven, to be sprinkled on by each guest. This sweet is suitable also for holiday luncheons or Sunday suppers. For 5–6 persons.[5]

Although some still believed that the old rules had to be followed just as inevitably as the fish course followed the soup, in 1937 no less an authority than Emily Post, the most important etiquette arbiter in America, wrote,

> It may be due to the war period, which accustomed everyone to going with very little meat and to marked reduction in all food, or it may be, of course, merely vanity that is causing even grand-parents to aspire to svelte figures, but whatever the cause, people are putting much less food on their tables than formerly. The very rich, living in the biggest houses with the most imposing array of servants, sit down to three, or at most four, courses when alone, or when intimate friends who are known to have moderate appetites are dining with them.[6]

Post went so far as to say that people need not worry about which fork to use. 'The choice of an implement is entirely unimportant – a trifling detail which people of high social position care nothing about.'[7] Her book, originally titled *Etiquette in Society, in Business, in Politics, and at Home*, was first published in 1922. Later retitled *Etiquette: 'The Blue Book of Social Usage'*, the guide went through ten editions and ninety printings before her death. She also wrote a syndicated news-paper column and had her own radio programme. Thousands of her readers and listeners wrote to her with their problems, questions and concerns, and she was wise enough to listen and respond. As a result, she was an excellent barometer. She was aware of the changes in their lives and with each new edition of her guide, she adapted the rules to reflect changing customs. Although Post did not mention it, this was also the era of the worldwide Great Depression, which was forcing many to reduce spending on food and everything else they could, whether they wished to or not.

Post realized that although fewer households had servants, women still wanted to entertain guests, so she offered strategies designed for

Pairing ice cream and wafers is traditional. Serving them in a cocktail glass is a more recent trend.

them. She dubbed them 'Mrs Three-in-One' because they had to be cook, waitress and 'a tranquil and apparently unoccupied hostess'. Post recommended buffets and even suggested keeping paper plates, cups and napkins on hand in case of unexpected guests.[8] However, Post's relaxed attitude towards forks and formality had its limits. Unlike Cole Porter, she did not believe that 'anything goes'. She had definite opinions on the appropriate dishes to serve for dessert, as well as on French chefs. She wrote,

The captious say, 'dessert means the fruit and candy which come after the ices.' 'Ices' is a misleading word, too, because in the present day the 'dessert' is ice cream, served in one mold; not ices (a lot of little frozen images). And the refusal to call the 'sweets' at the end of the dinner, which certainly include ice cream and cake, 'dessert,' is at least not the interpretation of either good usage or good society. In France, where the word 'dessert' originated, 'ices' were set apart from dessert merely because French chefs delight in designating each item of a meal as a separate course. But, chefs and cook-books not withstanding, dessert means everything sweet that comes at the end of a meal. And the great American dessert is ice cream – or pie. Pie, however, is not a 'company' dessert. Ice cream, on the other hand, is the inevitable conclusion of a formal dinner.[9]

In the 1922 edition, this paragraph concluded with the following statement: 'The fact that the spoon which is double the size of a teaspoon is known as nothing but a dessert spoon, is offered in further proof that "dessert" is "spoon" not "finger" food.'[10] When the 1937 edition was published, Post omitted the information about the spoon.

KEEPING COOL

At the time when Post was writing about the inevitability of ice cream, few people could afford a refrigerator. In the U.S. during the early 1920s, the price of a Model T Ford was $300, the annual household income averaged $2,000, and refrigerators cost about $900. Mass production of more reasonably priced refrigerators did not begin until after the Second World War. Most British households did not have a refrigerator until the 1960s. Earlier households kept food cold in iceboxes (which, confusingly, were often referred to as refrigerators) or cool cellars. If the weather was cold enough, city dwellers kept foods like ice cream on fire escapes; suburbanites would keep the foods on the back porch or under the snow in the back garden. In the 1975 edition of *Joy of Cooking*, author Irma S.

This 1870 advertisement is for an icebox, called here a 'refrigerator'.

Rombauer reminisced about the way her family stored moulded ice creams in winter when she was young: 'We children always hoped they might be chilled in the backyard, under snow: such fun finding them!'[11]

Refrigerator manufacturers realized that families needed to be convinced that the new appliance was worth the expense. One heading in a cookbook of 1927 published by the General Electric Company read, 'Why a refrigerator?' The writer recommended it for chilling ice bags for the sick as well as for keeping ice cream and other items frozen. This was despite that fact that the early refrigerators' freezing compartments were hardly larger than an ice cube tray. The booklet's author, identified as Miss Alice Bradley, Principal of Miss Farmer's School of Cookery, and Cooking Editor of *Woman's Home Companion*, was candid about the refrigerator's practicality. She wrote,

> As this book is being compiled the electric refrigerator is yet
> a new invention and the total sum of its usefulness has not in
> any way been discovered. It has proved that it is an immense
> improvement over the ice chest that has to be chilled by ice.
> It remains for the users of electric refrigerators to find new
> ways to make it serve them.[12]

As prices went down and more people could afford refrigerators, recipes in cookbooks and manufacturer's booklets helped users find those ways. The recipes included refrigerator cookies, refrigerator dough, refrigerator rolls, refrigerator cakes and more. Individuals who were fortunate enough to afford refrigerators made dishes to show them off. Hostesses froze fruits and flowers in ice cubes, unconsciously creating pale imitations of the impressive ice pyramids of seventeenth-century tables. The era of frozen salads, frozen cheese and, more happily, frozen mousses and parfaits began. As the English author Elizabeth David wrote,

In England at this time it was quite avant garde to possess
a refrigerator ... The thirties was the decade when smart
hostesses took to serving a great many dishes iced or frozen
simply for the originality of the idea.[13]

DESSERT IN WARTIME

It might seem trivial to speak of dessert during wartime, especially
during the Second World War and the post-war period, but a bit of
sweetness, whether actual or remembered, was welcomed in such bitter
times. The writer and art collector Gertrude Stein and her partner
Alice B. Toklas lived in France throughout the war, and Toklas later
wrote a cookbook-cum-memoir about the foods they had and those
they missed. The women had moved from Paris to Bligny, in northeast
France, during the German occupation. There, Toklas said, 'We lived
on our past.' More fortunate than most, they had a vegetable garden

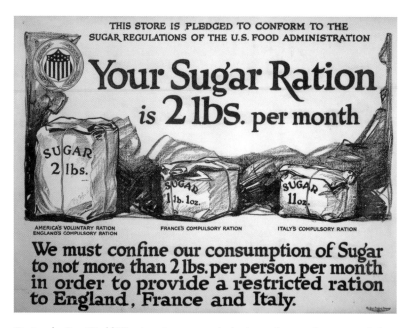

During the First World War, Americans were asked voluntarily to use less sugar to help
the English, French and Italians, who were restricted to using much less.

After seven years of rationing, these children in London could finally enjoy some sweets.

and wine in the cellar, but lacked butter, milk and eggs. When Toklas made a pseudo-flummery with raspberry jelly for dessert, she wrote, 'The flummery cried for cream. So did we.'[14]

It helped to look forward to the day when it would be possible to make a favourite dessert. Toklas treasured two glass jars filled with

raisins, candied citron, pineapple, cherries and orange and lemon peel
that she had obtained in 1940. Saying she was saving them for the
day when she could make a Liberation fruit cake, she wrote, 'They
cheered me greatly during the increasingly dismal days of that winter
and the early spring of 1944.'[15] When German soldiers were billeted
with them in the house in Bligny, Toklas hid the jars in the linen cup-
board. As soon as the soldiers left and France was liberated, she made
the cake.

In 1954, when Toklas wrote *The Alice B. Toklas Cook Book*, she
said, 'Even now French food has not yet returned to its old standard.'[16]
Rationing ended the same year in England, and for years afterwards,
certain foods remained scarce. Compared to Europe and England, the
U.S. was hardly touched by rationing or food scarcity. Sugar was
rationed but substitutes such as corn syrup, honey, molasses, maple
syrup and jelly were not. Manufacturers and home cooks alike used
marshmallows as a sweetener. They melted marshmallows and mixed
them with evaporated milk to make a variety of frozen desserts, which
they called marlobets, mallobets or marlows, and tossed marshmallows
into everything from salads to puddings.

The Depression and wars did have some impact on the way
Americans baked, not only at those times but afterwards. The following
fruit cake recipe was baked, modified and shared over many years.
Doris Luck Pullen, a writer and educator who lived in Lexington,
Massachusetts, made the cake for family and friends long after
Depression-era frugality and wartime rationing had ended. This is the
recipe she gave to friends, complete with her notes on its origins and
keeping qualities.

DORIS'S FRUITCAKE

This was a World War I eggless, butterless, milkless cake converted
into a holiday fruit cake. Originally, (without the candied fruits)
it was simply a spice cake, thus it has a different aspect from
traditional fruit cakes. The 'booze' can be brandy or rum, and

Light, puffy marshmallows sweetened many U.S. desserts when sugar was rationed during the Second World War.

brushed on in whatever quantity after the cakes have cooled. Tradition has it that it preserves the cakes well into the new year.

Stew 15 min.: 1 lb. raisins
2 c. water
Add: 1 T. baking soda
1 c. cold water
¼ lb. (1 stick) margarine
2 c. sugar
1 t. each of cloves, cinnamon, nutmeg, salt
Beat in: 4 c. flour, 1 jar (approximately one pound) fruits, nutmeats (optional).
Bake at 350° 45–60 min., depending on the size of pans & oven.
Will make 5 small loafpan cakes.
Brush with booze when cool, if desired.

M.F.K. Fisher, the American writer known for her literary and sensuous approach to food writing, included a recipe for a 'surprisingly good' war cake in *How to Cook a Wolf*, first published in 1942. The cake called for a half-cup of shortening, and Fisher noted that bacon grease could be used because the spices in the cake hid its taste. She suggested cinnamon and 'cloves, mace, ginger, etc.', along with chopped raisins or other dried fruits. She also recommended a dessert that might have been served during the Middle Ages, writing,

> Roast some walnuts in their shells, and eat them while they
> are still pretty hot, with fresh cold apples and a glass of port
> if possible, for one of the desserts most conducive in this world
> to good conversation.[17]

During the war, ice cream was banned in the UK and in Italy, but declared an essential food in the U.S., thanks to the lobbying of ice cream manufacturers. As a result, ice cream became a symbol of patriotism at home and a morale builder for troops overseas. U.S. manufacturers did have to make some concessions to wartime conditions: they churned out fewer flavours, owing to the dearth of some ingredients and to cut down on packaging and labour; they cut the butterfat content from about 14 per cent to 10 per cent and substituted corn syrup for some of the rationed sugar. The resulting ice cream was less rich, and U.S. ice-cream consumption increased during the war. In 1940 Americans ate just over 10 quarts (9.5 litres) of ice cream per capita; by 1945 they were consuming nearly 17 quarts (16 litres). Just a year later, consumption was slightly more than 20 quarts (18.9 litres).[18] Some of the compromises with ingredients continued after the war, not because of shortages or rationing, but because making ice cream with less butterfat and more air was more profitable. In the 1960s high-butterfat ice cream, referred to as superpremium but essentially the pre-war style with a new label, was introduced to the marketplace and became a hit.

Turning to Jelly

Today, colourful jiggly jellies delight children, mix with fruits and creams to form frothy desserts and lend support to such elegant dishes as Bavarian creams, mousses and cold soufflés. Artists sculpt with gelatine, teachers turn it into finger-paints, and some people wrestle in it. However, it was not until the nineteenth century that affordable, easy-to-use sheet and powdered gelatines were marketed in the UK and the U.S. The earliest ones were unreliable and unpopular, but when improved by added sugar and fruit flavours, powdered gelatines began to be accepted. In 1902 the Jell-O brand was advertised as 'America's Most Famous Dessert'.

During the Second World War, gelatine desserts were especially prized in the U.S., because, unlike sugar, gelatine was not rationed. The

By the turn of the 20th century, jellies had become easy and inexpensive to make, if not as impressive as they once were.

most popular brand, Jell-O, encouraged wartime sales with a booklet titled *Bright Spots for Wartime Meals: 66 Ration-wise Recipes*, which included both sweet and savoury dishes made with Jell-O. Eventually sugar rationing did force General Foods, the company behind the product, to cut back on production, and there were fewer packages of Jell-O on American grocery store shelves. Turning a problem into an opportunity, the company ran humorous ads, some by the *New Yorker* cartoonist Helen Hokinson, depicting clever ways women dealt with the scarcity of Jell-O.[19]

QUICK AND EASY

After the war, as Europeans coped with food shortages, the food industry was encouraging American women to make cakes and other desserts from mixes. They were quick, easy, time-saving solutions for the busy housewife, according to the advertising. It was true that women were busy. Many had jobs outside the home, and those who did not still had to live up to the responsibilities of 'Mrs Three-in-One', as Post had pointed out years earlier. More important, the mixes were lifesavers for the companies that produced flour, such as General Mills, General Foods and Pillsbury. Fewer women were baking their own bread, and the industry needed to compensate for the decline in flour sales. They promoted their cake, muffin and other mixes to solve the problem.

Shortcake made with stone fruit and a box of Miss Jones's cake mix.

Because some women felt guilty about taking such shortcuts, the industry promoted creative ways to use the mixes. They printed recipes on their packages as well as in pamphlets, cookbooks, magazines and newspapers, just as the gelatine companies had. Some mixes called for adding an egg to help women feel more involved in baking, but as the author Laura Shapiro pointed out in her comprehensive study of the era, *Something from the Oven: Reinventing Dinner in 1950s America* (2004), the mixes that included dried eggs were no less popular. 'Creativity was the fairy dust that would transform opening boxes into real cooking,' Shapiro explained.[20] Industry recipes promised magically to transform plain cakes into appealing desserts a homemaker could serve with pride. If a woman did not feel comfortable serving a simple yellow cake made from a packaged mix, she could top it with shop-bought ice cream, cover it with homemade meringue and brown it in the oven. It was easy to make, but it was nevertheless an impressive baked Alaska.

Not everyone wanted to use mixes, at least not all the time. The women who sent their recipes and suggestions to newspaper features like the *Boston Globe*'s 'Confidential Chat' prided themselves on baking desserts from scratch. The *Globe* had established a 'Housekeeper's Column' in 1884 and renamed it 'Confidential Chat' in 1922. Until it was discontinued in January 2006, this early form of crowd-sourcing offered people, both men and women (but with a preponderance of women), a place to share concerns, advice on relationships and, especially, recipes. They sent in recipes for their husband's favourite brownies, their children's special birthday cake and their mother's traditional pie. They answered each other's requests for recipes for everything from a cheesecake made without cheese to 'Gram Lynch's Gum Drop Cake'.[21] These women sometimes used mixes, but they preferred making desserts from scratch.

The *Better Homes and Gardens Dessert Cook Book*, published in 1960, included recipes for both possibilities and for most occasions. There were recipes for homey desserts such as apple dumplings and lemon meringue pie, along with detailed ones for puff pastry, choux paste and classic Napoleons, 'The ultimate in a French pastry-chef's art!'[22] The book featured a selection of '1-2-3 desserts' made with packaged foods to 'give you a head start'. A 'Glamorous Coffee-toffee Torte' was made with angel food cake mix, chocolate pudding mix, instant coffee, English toffee bars and whipped cream.[23] Instant puddings were flavoured with pineapple or apricot juice instead of milk, and enhanced with whipped cream to make a dessert that could be mixed up 'in a jiffy'.[24] Shop-bought ice cream was dressed up with frozen fruits, marshmallows, chocolate chips or corn flakes.

For years, cake mixes and ready-to-use products changed little. They seemed to be rooted in a distant past. However, early in the twenty-first century, new mixes debuted. Some are gluten-free; some contain no corn syrup, soy or dairy; while some are non-GMO (not containing genetically modified organisms). In short, they are intended for young cooks who want something quick and easy, but do not want artificial flavourings and unpronounceable chemicals in their baked goods. The newcomers call for added ingredients on the old theory that users want to be more involved in the process, and they also emphasize the fairy dust of creativity. The Immaculate Baking Company uses the term 'scratch baking mix' for mixes that call for the addition of eggs, milk and butter. The company's website shows how to transform the cake mixes into desserts such as 'Easy Chocolate

Using an instant pudding mix, anyone can make a lush lemon pie.

Individual cakes made with matcha tea and cake mix.

Ganache Zucchini Cake' and 'S'mores Fudgy Brownies'.[25] The Miss Jones Baking Co., launched in 2014, produces cake mixes and ready-to-use frostings that are certified organic. The company features recipes such as 'Rosé All Day Cake', 'Candied Negroni Cakelets' and 'Matcha Tea Cakes' on its website, and encourages customers to share their creations on social media.[26]

FRENCH REVOLUTIONS

In the 1960s Julia Child, through her books, newspaper columns and television programmes, showed Americans that cooking, even French cooking, could be pleasurable. In the foreword to her first book, *Mastering the Art of French Cooking*, published in 1961, she wrote,

> This is a book for the servantless American cook who can be unconcerned on occasion with budgets, waistlines, time schedules, children's meals, the parent-chauffeur-den-mother syndrome, or anything else which might interfere with the enjoyment of producing something wonderful to eat.[27]

Although her book was published just a year after the *Better Homes and Gardens Dessert Cook Book*, Child did not use mixes, admitted that cooking took time and, rather than offering quick and easy recipes, promised her readers dishes that would taste wonderful. Desserts were not Child's speciality, but the book included a selection of standard French classics such as chocolate mousse, *crêpes Suzette* and *reine de saba* (chocolate and almond cake). In subsequent books, she added many more, including a decidedly un-French Christmas plum pudding.

Whether they ever prepared any of her recipes or not, people responded to the warmth of Child's personality. She influenced the way people – from the aspiring cook, to the woman who relied on mixes, to the feminist who thought cooking was too fraught with second-sex associations – thought about cooking and eating. Child wanted Americans to enjoy cooking and to delight in dining, as she so clearly did. She concluded the foreword to *Mastering the Art of French Cooking* by writing, 'Above all, have a good time.'[28]

At the same time that Child was teaching Americans traditional French cooking techniques, French chefs in France were overturning tradition and spreading the gospel of nouvelle cuisine. It was inevitable. The 1960s and '70s were a time of cultural upheaval. University students were protesting; the anti-war and civil rights movements were intensifying; skirts grew ever shorter, hair longer; and young French chefs revolted. Chefs including Paul Bocuse, Jean and François Troisgros, Alain Chapel and Roger Vergé transformed and simplified their dishes and inspired others to do the same. The gastronomic writers Henri Gault and Christian Millau coined the term 'nouvelle cuisine' to describe the movement and championed its philosophy in their dining guides. The new approach was characterized by fresh seasonal ingredients, shorter menus, the elimination of the flour-based sauces that had been a French mainstay, and openness to new techniques and equipment. One of its most important hallmarks was individual, artistically arranged plating, influenced by Japanese art.

The upside-down apple tart called tarte Tatin is named for two sisters who popularized it at their Orléans inn in the 19th century. It became one of France's favourite desserts.

Although nouvelle cuisine was caricatured as merely small portions on big plates, it was the first important change in presentation since the nineteenth century when *service à la Russe* was introduced. Eventually nouvelle cuisine transformed culinary habits far beyond the borders of France.

Among their other achievements, the young chefs introduced humour to the language of menus. Traditional gourmets, who thought they spoke the language fluently, now discovered words had hitherto unknown meanings. Quenelles were not necessarily delicate dumplings of minced fish or meat; they might be similarly shaped mounds of ice cream. Marmalade could be made from onions as well as oranges. Millefeuilles might be the familiar flaky puff pastry layered with pastry cream, or they might be made from thin layers of potatoes. As a result, those who took pride in knowing the language no longer held an advantage over the novice who did not speak menu-French. The new vocabulary meant everyone had to learn, ask questions and engage in conversation with servers in a less formal, more democratic way.

Desserts became less ostentatious, fresher and more focused on seasonal fruits than elaborate cakes and pastries. The plated desserts were often garnished with fanciful sugar or chocolate decorations, but enormous head-turning presentations like Soyer's boar cake were no more. Nouvelle desserts – fresh peach soufflé, vanilla ice-cream quenelles scattered with fresh raspberries and served on a pool of delicate raspberry coulis, caramelized pear slices atop a disc of fragile puff pastry – were light and irresistible. In a *New Yorker* profile of

William Curley's contemporary version of Mont Blanc, the chestnut and whipped cream dessert named after the highest mountain in the Alps.

Michel Guérard, the writer Joseph Wechsberg described a dessert he ate at Le Pot au Feu, Guérard's restaurant in Paris, writing,

> I usually skip dessert but ... in a moment of weakness
> I ordered *granite de chocolat amer et brioche rôtie*. This was
> a sherbet consisting of finely crushed ice and bitter chocolate,
> and served with a hot, sweet brioche ... Guérard asked, 'Was
> it light enough?'[29]

The new style spread throughout Europe, the UK, America and beyond. In 1982 the author Anne Willan, then director of the prestigious La Varenne cooking school in Paris, reported, 'In the United States, every major city has one or more nouvelle-cuisine restaurants, and in France any establishment with an eye on its listings in the Michelin or Gault-Millau guides features the new style.'[30] The American author Raymond Sokolov, writing in *Natural History* magazine in 1983, said, 'The success of this new mode of cooking is a fact of contemporary life. Nouvelle cuisine triumphed in France and then radiated outward throughout Europe, to the United States, and back to Japan.'[31]

Its influence was felt in what came to be called New American cuisine, exemplified by Alice Waters. In her California restaurant, Chez Panisse, she cooked with the freshest ingredients and delighted in experimenting in both her savoury and her dessert dishes with produce local farmers introduced to her. In the UK, new chefs including Marco Pierre White, Gordon Ramsay and Fergus Henderson used nouvelle techniques and ideas to transform British dining. Not everyone used the words 'nouvelle cuisine', but nearly everyone adopted, or adapted, elements of the style. Flavourful and fresh triumphed over staid and pompous.

PLAYING WITH FOOD

For at least two centuries, the world of haute cuisine revolved around France. French chefs and pastry chefs set the styles and standards, and others followed. Historically, whether in Russia, England or Italy, those who were wealthy enough to do so hired French chefs and ate French foods. Restaurants all over the world presented menus written in French. Trends such as nouvelle cuisine were born in France.

Then, at the end of the twentieth century, the food world tilted on its axis and its centre became a restaurant called El Bulli, located in a remote village in Spain. There two brothers, Ferran and Albert Adrià, chef and pastry chef respectively, pioneered and publicized a dramatic new cuisine. In 2003 a *New York Times Magazine* cover story made it official. The headline read, 'The Nueva Nouvelle Cuisine: How Spain Became the New France'. When chef and author Anthony Bourdain saw the brothers' book, *A Day at el Bulli*, he said, 'Pastry chefs everywhere – when they see this – will gape in fear, and awe, and wonder. I feel for them . . . one imagines they will ask themselves "What do I do now?"'[32]

Strudel means 'whirlpool', and a traditional apple strudel is awhirl with pastry, apples, cinnamon, raisins and flavour.

At the Amorino gelato shop in Barcelona, ice cream is swirled into cones to form fanciful flower-like petals.

Variously called 'modernist cuisine', 'molecular gastronomy', 'constructivist' or 'avant-garde cuisine', the style combines chemistry, physics and cooking. Its equipment is borrowed from the science lab; its ingredients from the food industry or the pharmacy. Its chefs use centrifuges, dehydrators and syringes, along with whisks, bowls and sheet pans. They work with ingredients like sodium alginate, xanthan gum, dextrose powder and tapioca maltodextrin, as well as eggs, flour, sugar and vanilla beans. They use techniques such as dehydration and spherification, as well as creaming and baking. The result is food that dazzles the eyes and surprises the taste buds.

After earning three Michelin stars, El Bulli closed in 2011 with promises of reopening someday. However, its influence continued to spread. It could be found in restaurants such as Heston Blumenthal's The Fat Duck in England, Wylie Dufresne's WD-50 in New York, Grant Achatz's Alinea in Chicago, Pierre Gagnaire's eponymous restaurant in Paris and Rene Redzepi's Noma in Copenhagen. The sophisticated new techniques are not limited to any country or cuisine. They span the globe. Books, seminars, university courses and especially websites and blogs all disseminate information about the practice.

Modernist desserts are fanciful, exotic, trompe l'oeil triumphs that might look like anything from branches of coral to mossy gardens to guitar amplifiers. Chefs use 3-D printers to make sugar or chocolate sculptures. They make foams of fruits and solid bubbles of cocoa and milk, and turn chocolate-covered cherries into cherry-covered chocolates. Unlikely ice-cream flavours are one of the chefs' favourite playthings. That in itself is nothing new. In the eighteenth century, Vincenzo Corrado wrote that talented confectioners could turn any vegetable into a sorbet. So making ice cream with beetroot, tonka beans or shiso leaves as chefs do now is not particularly exotic, although flavouring it with tobacco smoke is a departure.

Using liquid nitrogen to freeze ice cream is not new either, but it is more widespread than ever before. Mrs Agnes Marshall had mentioned the possibility in 1901, although it is doubtful that she actually did it, since her description of the process was flawed and would not have worked. But she did realize that it was possible and suggested that it would entertain dinner guests. A century later, she was proved right. Chefs in fine-dining restaurants entertained guests by using the technique to create custom-flavoured ice creams à la minute.

Freezing with liquid nitrogen is also used in down-to-earth venues. Recently young entrepreneurs in Cambridge, Massachusetts, turned a shipping container into an ice-cream shop called Churn2.

Using liquid nitrogen adds drama, as well as speed, to ice-cream making.

They made custom ice creams using liquid nitrogen, much to the delight of customers young and old. The shipping container was parked, appropriately, just outside Harvard University's Science Center.

Home cooks who want to try creating new desserts with modernist techniques can find equipment and recipes online, buy a whipping siphon and some nitrous oxide canisters, and make what is said to be a 'fluffy, impressive dessert from boxed cake mix in about a minute in the microwave'. They can buy calcium lactate gluconate, sodium alginate and a silicone mould, and use a technique called 'frozen reverse spherification' to transform carrot, orange and mango juices into a shape that looks like an egg yolk and serve it surrounded by rose crystals.[33] The possibilities are limitless for anyone with the time and wherewithal to experiment.

OUT OF BOUNDS

Not everyone wants to transform kitchens into chemistry labs, and not every dessert menu is meant to be innovative. Some restaurateurs cannot afford the investment in new equipment; others know cutting-edge desserts are not what their clientele wants. Hotels, bakeries and restaurants all have different customers with their own preferences. As a result, the role of the dessert chef varies greatly today. In the seventeenth century, the duties of a chef and a pastry chef were strictly delineated. The chef prepared, or supervised, the savoury courses; the pastry chef worked in the *office*, or cold kitchen, and prepared the sweet desserts, cold dishes and sugar sculptures. In the twenty-first century, these distinctions are no longer so distinct. The strict boundaries of the French kitchen have become less restrictive.

In many restaurants, chefs create the desserts themselves, some-times to avoid the expense of a pastry chef, sometimes because they enjoy it. They often incorporate ingredients formerly considered suitable only for savoury dishes into their desserts. Pastry chefs have different specialities depending on where they work. Those who are employed in restaurants make individual plated desserts rather than the large-scale cakes and impressive displays that are the province of pastry chefs in hotels and banquet facilities. Some pastry chefs con-sult for two or three different restaurants, creating the dessert menus but leaving it up to the cooks to prepare the dishes. Restaurants with conventional dinner menus generally stay with the tried and true on their dessert menus. Their pastry chefs might pay tribute to a mythical mum by offering diners choices like a plate of freshly baked biscotti or gingerbread, or specialize in seasonal desserts such as fruit tarts in summer, or crème brûlée or chocolate pudding in winter. Restaurants that cater to a sophisticated clientele have to offer more inventive dishes, like a flight of tiny, similarly flavoured desserts. For example, they might serve espresso mousse swirled atop a miniature mocha sponge cake, alongside chocolate ganache ribbons, and a scoop of white chocolate ice cream topped with coffee foam. They emphasize artistic plating as well as taste.

Retail pastry shops offer individual desserts such as macarons and cupcakes as well as pies and cakes. Chocolatiers, who specialize in technically demanding chocolate creations, more often work in or own shops rather than restaurants, though they may be called on to create elaborate sculptures for banquets. Pastry chefs who work for food service companies create desserts that can be mass-produced.

Many in the restaurant business find it more convenient and profitable to outsource their desserts to a food service company than to employ a pastry chef. The desserts arrive frozen, ready to thaw and serve, or briefly bake or microwave and serve. The range of products is vast. *Petits fours*, apple tarts, mousse cakes, brownies, puddings – all sorts of desserts are prepared, frozen and shipped around the country or the world for sale. Sometimes called the 'invisible frozen items', they are delivered to restaurants, hotels, bakeries and catering services, and then sold to consumers who may not realize that the cheesecake or éclair they are enjoying was not made on the premises, but transported long distances to their plates.[34] (Of course, such desserts can also be found in supermarket freezers, where such information is visible and clearly labelled).

Frozen desserts are made and sold everywhere from Tokyo to Dallas, from Paris to London. The companies that make the desserts pride themselves on their quality, creativity and value. The *European Food Journal*, a trade publication, quoted a representative of the French company Boncolac as saying,

> We have a team of passionate chefs and patissiers who love baking and are well aware of the tradition of French pastry making . . . We devise sophisticated recipes. However, we have developed state-of-the-art production processes that help us preserve all the flavours before the food products are frozen.[35]

Dianne's Fine Desserts, a U.S. company, calls itself 'The Creators of the Ultimate Expression of a Fine Dessert' and promises to help 'build your dessert business one delighted customer at a time'.[36] The UK's Dessert Company explains that it provides

> a wide range of luxury pre-prepared desserts for the catering trade. Competitively priced to allow maximum room for profit margins, including the savings made on preparation time as well, we top it all off with fast and reliable delivery service. Desserts sorted.[37]

Still, consumers would likely appreciate it if the origins of the products were not quite so invisible.

Something Old, Something New

In 1549 a feast was held in Binche castle in Belgium in honour of Philip II of the Netherlands. The event was held in the *salle enchantée*, a magical room with a ceiling decorated with stars in the form of lamps burning perfumed oil. Tables bearing an elaborate sugar banquet descended from the ceiling accompanied by the sound of thunder and a hail of *dragées délicieuses*.[38]

In 2015 a table descended from the ceiling of chef Dominique Ansel's New York restaurant, Dominque Ansel Kitchen, for the first on a series of after-hours dessert tastings called U. P., for Unlimited Possibilities. Serving just eight guests and comprised of eight courses, the initial tasting menu was composed on the theme of 'First Memories Last Forever'. Courses included 'First Word', a variation on a floating island with flavours that recalled baby's first foods. The crème anglaise was made with vanilla-infused sweet pea rice milk, and in lieu of baby's strained carrots, small squares of carrot cake floated atop the custard. Another course, 'First Heartbreak', included Rocky Road ice cream surrounded by meringue petals. The guests were invited to set the petals aflame to melt the ice cream, just as first loves often blaze and then melt away.[39]

Some of today's best-known dessert chefs delight in reinterpreting or deconstructing traditional desserts to make innovative contemporary versions. The Scottish chef and four-time winner of Best British Chocolatier by the Academy of Chocolate William Curley is known for reimagining old favourites, such as Black Forest cake. Rather than baking one large chocolate and cherry cake, he makes small individual cakes. Each one is comprised of chocolate sponge cake, kirsch syrup, chocolate mousse, cherry compote and chocolate wafers. He freezes the cakes, and then covers them with a glistening chocolate glaze. They appear quite simple on the surface, but inside is a complex blend of flavours and textures.[40]

Jean-François Deguignet, Le Cordon Bleu Paris Institute Technical Director–Pastry, has created miniature versions of the

Perhaps inspired by the apple trees in his Giverny garden, Claude Monet painted classic, timeless French tarts.

traditional Paris-Brest. Made from choux paste as the original is, his small spheres sit atop discs of shortbread and white chocolate. The pastries are filled with a Japanese-influenced mango, passion fruit and yuzu coulis and chocolate cream, and then frozen. He pours a white chocolate glaze tinted yellow-green over the small domes and decorates them with a tiny bit of silver leaf. The techniques are traditional, the ingredients are international, and the interpretation is his alone.[41]

Whether based on older creations or new ideas, dessert trends know no boundaries. One of the ways they are transmitted is an old one – pastry competitions. Competitions date back at least to nineteenth-century Paris, and spread to London, Vienna and other cities. Today, teams of pastry chefs from countries all over the world gather in various locations to compete for honours and prizes. They come from France,

William Curley, British pâtissier-chocolatier, gives his Black Forest cakes a sleek new look, but retains the flavours of the original.

the UK, Japan, Korea, the U.S., Germany and elsewhere to spend up to four days demonstrating their skill, creativity and stamina. The categories include sugar sculpture, marzipan modelling, plated desserts, *petits fours*, chocolate showpieces, frozen desserts, verrines (layered desserts presented in glass) and entremets. Entremets, no longer dishes or entertainments served between courses, are now desserts. The judges, internationally known dessert professionals, score entries on artistry, technical merit and taste. In addition to offering financial rewards and prestige, the contests spark ideas, introduce chefs to new ingredients and spread knowledge. Televised competitions, whether involving professionals or amateurs, are not only exciting to watch but increase viewers' knowledge and raise their dessert expectations. Ultimately, competitions lead to new experiences and taste sensations for dessert lovers.

Soyer and Escoffier might not have recognized the techniques, equipment or even many of the ingredients chefs use today, but they would have delighted in the drama and playfulness of the creations. Carême, master of the architectural dessert, would have been amazed at the 3-D printers that create today's sugar sculptures. Emy would probably have been sceptical about freezing ice cream with liquid nitrogen. After all, he did not approve of adding liqueurs to ice cream. But if he had tried it, he might have been impressed and added the new technique to his repertoire. Today's pastry chefs are part of a long continuum of chefs who are always trying to make their mark in new and taste-tempting ways.

DESSERT MAKES A HOLIDAY

Holiday desserts have a special place in our hearts. They may be old-fashioned. We may not have them at any other time of year. We may not even like them much. But, depending on our tradition, we must have our pumpkin pie at Thanksgiving, our Christmas (or plum) pudding at Christmas, our baklava during Ramadan or our sweet cheese *sandesh* for Diwali.

Making, and anticipating, the Thanksgiving pie, on the cover of *Puck* magazine (1903).

If a traditional holiday dessert is banned, it becomes more cherished. Not even a Communist dictator can keep us from enjoying it. When Albena Shkodrova, now a writer living in Belgium, was growing up in Bulgaria under Communism, celebrating Christmas was forbidden. So her mother made *tikvenik*, their favourite Christmas dessert, for New Year's Eve. Going without it was not an option.

Tikvenik is a pastry filled with sweetened pumpkin and walnuts, spiced with cinnamon, and baked until crisp and golden. Part of the Shkodrova family's tradition was to insert fortunes written on small slips of paper into each pastry. Unfortunately, and often hilariously, Albena's mother was so tired after she had made all the holiday preparations and written all the fortunes that sometimes the pastries were not served to the appropriate person. One year, seven-year-old Albena was promised a professorship before the summer and a baby cousin was told he could expect a business trip to an exotic destination soon. But it was the *tikvenik* that mattered, and its fragrance as it baked still recreates the feeling of home and holidays for Shkodrova. She shared her family's recipe:

TIKVENIK

1 package of ready-made filo dough (you may not need it all), thawed

1 kg grated pumpkin or a 1-lb can of pumpkin purée (not pumpkin pie filling)

1 cup (150 g) coarsely chopped walnuts

⅓ cup (65 g) granulated sugar

2 teaspoons cinnamon

4 tablespoons rapeseed (canola) oil, approximately

icing (confectioners') sugar

Be sure to keep the filo dough that you're not using covered with a slightly damp cloth. Preheat the oven to 175°C (350°F). Oil a sheet pan or line with parchment.

In a bowl, stir the pumpkin, walnuts, sugar and cinnamon together.

Spread out one sheet of filo dough and spread a small amount of oil over it. Top with a second sheet of dough.

Spread one tablespoon of the filling over the dough, but avoid reaching the edges.

Roll it into a small tube and place in pan. Repeat until you've used all of the filling. Brush a little oil over the top of the *tikvenik* rolls.

Bake for 25 to 30 minutes, until crisp and brown.

Sprinkle with some confectioners' sugar and serve warm or at room temperature.

Makes about a dozen rolls.

Biscuits, or cookies, are ubiquitous in many countries at Christmastime. From Russia to Germany, from Italy to Spain, from France to the U.S., biscuits shaped and decorated to look like Saint Nicholas, Christmas trees, stars and gingerbread men are baked, exchanged and hung on Christmas trees. Many families have a traditional favourite. Emily Beck, a PhD candidate at the University of Minnesota, says the simple sugar cookies her grandmother made still mean Christmas to her, and 'they still taste best out of the giant green Tupperware bowl that she used for years!'[42]

Struffoli, deep-fried pastry balls dipped in honey, are a quintessential Neapolitan Christmas dessert. Rose Yesu, an educator from the Boston area, said that when she and her sisters were young, they could not wait for dessert. They held tea parties with their dolls and ate all the *struffoli* their mother would allow. Yesu's mother did not use a recipe, and her daughters never learned how she made them. Today, they look to recipes from friends, cookbooks or the Internet. But Yesu says, 'they never taste quite the same.'

In France, Quebec and other French-speaking regions, Christmas calls for the *bûche de Noël*, a cream-filled, rolled sponge cake that is covered with chocolate and meant to look like the log that brought warmth and light during winter's darkness. In Provence, there is the delightful practice of offering thirteen different sweets for dessert. Said to represent Christ and the twelve Apostles, they include a variety of fruits, nuts, nougat, cakes and biscuits.

The bread pudding known as *Mohnpielen* is a traditional German Christmas dessert. Ursula Heinzelmann, author of *Beyond Bratwurst* (2014), says that Christmas would be 'unthinkable' without a big bowl of the *Mohnpielen* her mother, and her mother before her, always made. Her maternal grandfather brought the recipe with him when he moved to Berlin from the former Eastern province of Silesia. Heinzelmann says that many families served the comforting mixture of bread, poppy seeds, raisins and milk to children after church on Christmas Eve 'as a calming prelude amongst the great excitement of the presents'. However, in her family it is served as Christmas dinner dessert, accompanied by a sweet Riesling.

In my family, after our Christmas dessert, we always linger over fruit, nuts and torrone or pizzelle. Growing up, I had no idea that the tradition harked back to the Middle Ages. Now that I do, I appreciate it even more.

Rosh Hashanah, the Jewish New Year, is observed in autumn and, in the Ashkenazi tradition, honey cake symbolizes the hope that the coming year will be sweet. Some say Rosh Hashanah without honey cake just would not be Rosh Hashanah. Then they admit that they don't like it. A friend who prefers to remain anonymous insists, 'No one likes honey cake.' She says they make or buy the cake, eat a few slices and wait for it to get stale enough to discard. Fruit cake plays the same role at Christmas for some.

Passover, the Jewish springtime holiday, has strict rules that deny cooks the use of regular flour and leavened or fermented foods. However, over time creative cooks have risen to the challenge with flourless tortes, coconut macaroons, meringues, chocolate-covered matzo and a lovely Italian almond and lemon sponge cake called *bocca di dama*, or lady's mouth. Despite the restrictions, Lawrence Newhouse, owner of a piano restoration business in California, says he loves Passover desserts. One of his favourites is a delectable dessert of unknown provenance and intriguing name that is more like a mousse-topped cake than a pie:

DARKNESS IN EGYPT CHOCOLATE MOUSSE PIE

200 g butter*

200 g sugar

2 tablespoons cocoa

100 g bittersweet chocolate

1 tablespoon brandy

4 eggs, separated**

4 tablespoons matzo meal

2 tablespoons walnuts, chopped

Preheat oven to 175°C (350°F). Butter a pie plate. Melt butter, sugar, cocoa and chocolate. Cool. Mix in the lightly whisked egg yolks and brandy.

Separately, beat egg whites until stiff and then fold them into the cooled chocolate mixture.

To one cup of the chocolate mixture, add the matzo meal. Pour that mixture into a buttered pie pan (reserve the rest) and bake for 30 minutes. Let cool.

Frost with reserved chocolate mixture, sprinkle with nuts, and serve.

* Use margarine rather than butter to make it pareve.
** The egg whites will not be cooked. If that's a concern, you may want to substitute pasteurized egg whites.

Spring is the season of awakening and renewal and of both religious and secular celebrations around the world. In the days before year-round everything and seasonless eating, spring meant more food was available. Winter had finally ended, and the earth was coming

alive with promising green sprouts. Animals gave birth, so there was a
renewed supply of eggs and milk. Today, although we take such ingredients for granted, we still serve desserts and sweets featuring eggs,
milk and cheese in spring. For some, that means giving chocolate eggs
and marshmallow chicks to children, who seldom know the meaning
behind the treats but are happy to gobble them up anyway. For me, it
means making my late Aunt Pansy Manzella's ricotta pie. It is a traditional Italian Easter dessert, but everyone makes his own version.
I spoke to a woman in a bakery in Puglia about the pie once, and she
asked if my family made it with wheat berries. I said that we did not.
Doesn't matter, she replied smiling, '*simile*'. This is my aunt's recipe.
I increased the amount of candied citron.

RICOTTA PIE
Line two 8- or 9-in (20-cm) pie plates with your favourite piecrust.
Preheat oven to 325°F (175°C).

2 lb (900 g) full-fat ricotta cheese
1 cup (200 g) sugar
4 large eggs
2 teaspoons anise (or vanilla) extract
3 tablespoons candied citron or orange peel

In a large bowl, using an electric mixer, beat ricotta and sugar until
very smooth. Add the eggs one at a time, beating well after each
addition. Mix in the extract and candied peel.

Pour into the pastry-lined pie pans and bake until set, about 35
minutes. Let cool. Sifting a little icing (confectioners') sugar over
the pie before serving is a nice touch.

Greek Orthodox Easter desserts also feature eggs and cheese.
Several years ago, in late May, in the village of Tochi in Cyprus, a local
woman offered to demonstrate how she made *flaounes*, the traditional

Cypriot Easter pastry. The pastries are filled with a mixture of halloumi (a Cypriot cheese), mint, sugar and usually raisins. We were excited to watch her make them and to taste them, but not as excited as her husband. He said this was the first time he had had *flaounes* twice in one year. His face was one big smile from the moment she began until long after the last *flaoune* was eaten.

Their connection to happy times, to family celebrations and to our memories are among the reasons that holiday desserts are treasured. And, perhaps, making them just once a year (and on a rare occasion, such as having visitors from another country) makes us cherish them even more.

TIME FOR DESSERT

There has never been a better time for those of us who think the last course is the best course. Whether we make our own desserts or buy them, we have ingredients, equipment and options that the wealthiest people of the past could not have imagined. We can conclude our meals with sweet wine, glazed nuts and dried fruits just as our medieval ancestors did. We can enjoy an old-time dessert like sticky toffee pudding or experiment with the new and make an airy mango and coconut foam with our whipping siphon. We can freeze ice cream with the press of a button rather than the tedious turning of a crank. We can bake a cherry pie or buy one.

Those who want to learn how to make desserts have a plethora of opportunities to do so. Recipes are more detailed and explicit than they once were, and books, magazines and newspapers are filled with them. Cooking shows on television and videos online demonstrate how to make everything from puff pastry to *petits fours*. All of the necessary, and sometimes not-so-necessary, equipment is available at the tap of a computer key. As the world grows smaller, recipes and ideas fly through the ether from country to country and reach everyone almost instantly.

Mohr im Hend (Moor in a Shirt), an individual chocolate cake robed in chocolate and crowned with whipped cream. No wonder Vienna is famed for desserts.

Life is also better for most of those who make their living by making our desserts. Although salaries are not always all they should be, pastry or dessert chefs are now treated as professionals. They may be female or male, and they may be from any country on earth. Chefs such as Soyer were prominent in the past, but most laboured in obscurity and often in difficult and unhealthy conditions. Today they are respected, and some are named on restaurant menus, profiled in magazines and newspapers, and featured on television and social media.

Over the centuries, the rules of dining etiquette have become more and more relaxed. Today, we are free to have the kind and style of dessert we choose. We can serve it on our most elegant china and decorate our table with a bouquet of roses, or call it a picnic and use paper plates. Our dessert can be a proper course with assigned seating, an informal buffet or a potluck. We can eat it with a fork, a spoon or our fingers.

ARTISTICALLY SERVED ICES.

1. Asparagus Ice flavoured with Asparagus Flavouring.
2. Violet Ice flavoured with Violet Flavouring and studded with Crystallized Violets.
3. Bunches of Roses, Violets, Primroses, Carnations, Orange Blossoms dressed with Ivy Leaves.
4. Three different Roses, also flavoured as Flowers.
5. Strawberry, Lemon, Raspberry, Chocolate, Cafe au Lait, Orange.

Elegant ices in 19th-century England from the famed *Encyclopædia of Practical Cookery.*

Best of all, desserts are more affordable and available to more people than ever before. While some of us are more fortunate than others, most can now afford to conclude dinner with something sweet. The ice cream is no longer reserved for the king's table. Everyone can have some. Dessert's time has arrived.

REFERENCES

ONE OUR ANCIENT EATING HABITS

1 Eileen Power, *The Goodman of Paris* (New York, 1928), p. 226, p. 173.
2 Nicole Crossley-Holland, *Living and Dining in Medieval Paris* (Cardiff, 1996), p. 163.
3 Rachel Laudan, *Cuisine and Empire: Cooking in World History* (Berkeley, CA, 2013), p. 177.
4 Jessica Mudry, 'Sugar and Health', in *The Oxford Companion to Sugar and Sweets*, ed. Darra Goldstein (New York, 2015), p. 671.
5 Kate Colquhoun, *Taste: The Story of Britain Through Its Cooking* (New York, 2007), Kindle edition unpaginated.
6 Anonymous, *Good Huswifes Handmaide, for the Kitchin* (London, 1594), p. 32.
7 Gervase Markham, *The English Housewife Containing the inward and outward Vertues which ought to be in a compleate Woman* (London, 1631), p. 107.
8 Anonymous, *Good Huswifes Handmaide*, pp. 31–2.
9 Terrence Scully, ed. and trans., *Chiquart's 'On Cookery': A Fifteenth-century Savoyard Culinary Treatise* (New York, 1986), pp. 17, 61.
10 Thomas Dawson, *The Good huswifes jewell* (London, 1587), p. 13.
11 Kate Atkinson, *Life After Life* (New York, 2013), p. 450.
12 Jean-Louis Flandrin, *Arranging the Meal: A History of Table Service in France* (Berkeley, CA, 2007), pp. 103–4.
13 Ephraim Chambers, *Cyclopaedia: Or an Universal Dictionary of Arts and Sciences* (London, 1741), unpaginated, https://books.google.com, accessed 31 August 2016.
14 Massimo Montanari, *Cheese, Pears, and History* (New York, 2010), p. 52.
15 Ibid., p. 8.
16 Elizabeth Field, *Marmalade: Sweet and Savory Spreads for a Sophisticated Taste* (Philadelphia, PA, 2012), p. 25.

17 Alan and Jane Davidson, trans., *Dumas on Food: Recipes and Anecdotes from the Classic Grand Dictionnaire de Cuisine* (Oxford, 1987), p. 210.

18 Mireille Johnston, *The Cuisine of the Sun* (New York, 1979), p. 238.

19 Power, *The Goodman of Paris*, pp. 305–6.

20 John Florio, *Queen Anna's New World of Words, or Dictionarie of the Italian and English Tongues* (London, 1611), p. 385, www.pbm.com, accessed 15 February 2016.

21 William Younger, *Gods, Men, and Wine* (Cleveland, OH, 1966), p. 284.

22 Ibid., p. 340.

23 Thomas Heywood, *The Fair Maid of the West* (London, 1631), https://archive.org, unpaginated, accessed 31 August 2016.

24 Hannah Woolley, *The Queene-like Closet or Rich Cabinet: Stored with All Manner of Rare Receipts For Preserving, Candying and Cookery. Very Pleasant and Beneficial to all Ingenious Persons of the Female Sex* (London, 1684), pp. 106–8.

25 In Shakespeare's *Henry IV, Part 1*, Hotspur scolds his wife Kate for swearing like a comfit-maker's wife. He means that her language is too refined. During Elizabethan times, lusty swearing was looked on approvingly, and Hotspur wanted her to swear 'a good mouth-filling oath'.

26 Sir Walter Scott, *The Journal of Sir Walter Scott* (New York, 1891), https://archive.org, unpaginated, accessed 28 November 2016.

27 Johann Wolfgang von Goethe, *Italian Journey*, trans. Robert R. Heitner (New York, 1989), pp. 402–4.

28 Charles Dickens, *Pictures from Italy* (Boston, MA, 1868), pp. 116–20.

TWO EATING WITH OUR EYES

1 Terrence Scully, 'The Mediaeval French *Entremets*', *Petits Propos Culinaires*, XVII (Totnes, 1984), pp. 44–56.

2 Marcia Reed, 'Feasting in the Streets', in *The Edible Monument: The Art of Food for Festivals,* ed. Marcia Reed (Los Angeles, CA, 2015), pp. 90–91.

3 Robert May, *The Accomplisht Cook, or the Art & Mystery of Cookery* (London, 1685), pp. 11–12.

4 Colin Spencer, *British Food: An Extraordinary Thousand Years of History* (London, 2001), p. 131.

5 Anonymous, *A Closet for Ladies and Gentlewomen. Or, The Art of Preserving, Conserving, and Candying* (London, 1611), pp. 30–34 and 39.

6 Gervase Markham, *The English Housewife* (London, 1631), p. 136.

7 Kathleen Curtin, 'Gervase Markham', in *Culinary Biographies*, ed. Alice Arndt (Houston, TX, 2006), pp. 254–5.

8 Markham, *The English Housewife*, p. 125.

9 Joseph Imorde, 'Edible Prestige', in *The Edible Monument: The Art of Food for Festivals*, ed. Marcia Reed (Los Angeles, CA, 2015), pp. 106–9.

10 Marcia Reed, 'Court and Civic Festivals', in *The Edible Monument: The Art of Food for Festivals*, ed. Marcia Reed (Los Angeles, CA, 2015), pp. 29–32.

11 Peter Brears, *Food and Cooking in 17th Century Britain: History and Recipes* (Birmingham, 1985), pp. 24–5.

12 Mary Işin, *Sherbet and Spice: The Complete Story of Turkish Sweets and Desserts* (London, 2013), pp. 52–7.

13 Tor Eigeland, 'Arabs, Almonds, Sugar and Toledo', *Saudi Aramco World* (Houston, TX, 1996), pp. 32–9.

14 Anonymous, *The Compleat Cook: Expertly prescribing the most ready ways, whether Italian, Spanish, or French, For dressing of Flesh, and Fish, ordering of Sauces or making of Pastry* (London, 1659), pp. 116–17.

15 Sir Kenelme Digby, *The Closet of the Eminently Learned Sir Kenelme Digby Kt. Opened* (London, 1671), pp. 213–14.

16 Jane Stevenson and Peter Davidson, eds, Introduction in *The Closet of Sir Kenelm Digby Opened* (Totnes, 1997), p. 31.

17 Digby, *The Closet*, p. 134.

18 Peter Brears, 'Rare Conceits and Strange Delightes: The Practical Aspects of Culinary Sculpture', in *Banquetting Stuffe*, ed. C. Anne Wilson (Edinburgh, 1991), p. 61.

19 William Rabisha, *The Whole Body of Cookery Dissected, Taught, and fully manifested Methodically, Artificially, and according to the best Tradition of the English, French, Italian, Dutch, &c.* (London, 1673), p. 269.

20 Digby, *The Closet*, p. 142.

21 T. Hall, *The Queen's Royal Cookery*, 2nd edn (London, 1713), pp. 166–70.

22 Digby, *The Closet*, pp. 247–8.

23 Darra Goldstein, 'Implements of Easting', in *Feeding Desire: Design and the Tools of the Table* (New York, 2006), p. 118.

24 Barbara Ketcham Wheaton, *Savouring the Past: The French Kitchen and Table from 1300 to 1789* (London, 1983), p. 163.

25 Anne Willan with Mark Cherniavsky and Kyri Claflin, *The Cookbook Library* (Berkeley, CA, 2012), pp. 166–7.

26 Nicola Humble, *Cake: A Global History* (London, 2010), p. 32.

27 François Massialot, *The Court and Country Cook*, trans. J. K. (London, 1702), p. 2.

28 François Massialot, 'New Instructions for Confectioners', in *The Court and Country Cook*, trans. J. K. (London, 1702), pp. 1–130.

29 Bartolomeo Stefani, *L'arte di ben cucinare, et instruire* (Mantua, 1662), pp. 119–27.

30 Wheaton, *Savouring the Past*, p. 188.

31 Charles Carter, *The Compleat City and Country Cook: or Accomplish'd Housewife* (London, 1732), pp. iii–viii.

32 Arthur Young, *Travels during the Years 1787, 1788, and 1789, Undertaken more particularly with a View of ascertaining the Cultivation, Wealth, Resources, and National Prosperity of the Kingdom of France* (Dublin, 1793), pp. 580–81.

33 Michael Krondl, 'Dessert', in *The Oxford Companion to Sugar and Sweets,* ed. Darra Goldstein (New York, 2015), pp. 212–13.

34 Ian Kelly, *Cooking for Kings: The Life of the First Celebrity Chef* (New York, 2003), pp. 192–4.

35 Anonymous, *The Whole Duty of a Woman, Or, an infallible Guide to the Fair Sex* (London, 1737), pp. 625–30.

36 Alexis Soyer, *The Modern Housewife or Ménagère* (London, 1851), p. 398.

37 Mrs W. M. Ramsay [Lady Agnes Dick (Marshall) Ramsay], *Every-day Life in Turkey* (London, 1897), pp. 150–55.

38 Lady Ramsay was mistaken, as was Lady Mary Wortley Montagu, who wrote in a letter from Adrianople dated April 1718, that soup was always the last dish of a Turkish dinner. She did not mention sweets. However, neither soup nor pilaf was necessarily the last dish. It was more often fruit. Lady Montagu's letter was published in *Turkish Embassy Letters* (London, 1993), pp. 87–8.

THREE Delights from the Dairy

1 Carolin Young 'La Laiterie de la Reine at Rambouillet', in *Milk: Beyond the Dairy: Proceedings of the Oxford Symposium on Food and Cookery, 1999,* ed. Harlan Walker (Blackawton, Devon, 2000), pp. 361–2.

2 Meredith Martin, *Dairy Queens: The Politics of Pastoral Architecture from Catherine de Medici to Marie-Antoinette* (Cambridge, MA, 2011), pp. 29–31, 186.

3 Ashlee Whitaker, 'Dairy Culture: Industry, Nature and Liminality in the Eighteenth-century English Ornamental Dairy' (2008), paper 1327, http://scholarsarchive.byu.edu, accessed 2 March 2016.

4 Isabella Beeton, *The Book of Household Management* (London, 1861), Entry 2358, www.gutenberg.org, accessed 28 March 2019.

5 Mary Eales, *Mrs Mary Eales's Receipts* (London, 1985), pp. 80–93. Facsimile of the 1733 edition; originally published in 1718.

6 François Massialot, *The Court and Country Cook* (London, 1702), pp. 93–7.

7 Ibid., p. 97.

8 Ardashes H. Keoleian, *The Oriental Cook Book: Wholesome, Dainty and Economical Dishes of the Orient, especially adapted to American Tastes and Methods of Preparation* (New York, 1913), p. 287. The author, who is identified only as 'Formerly of Constantinople', wrote that nationalities of his 'Orient' were Armenians, Bulgarians, Caucasians, Egyptians, Greeks, Jews, Persians, Syrians, Turks, etc.

9 E. Donald Asselin, *A Portuguese-American Cookbook* (Rutland, VT, 1966), p. 31.

10 C. Anne Wilson, *Food and Drink in Britain From the Stone Age to the 19th Century* (Chicago, IL, 1991), p. 173.

11 Elizabeth Raffald, *The Experienced English Housekeeper* [1769] (Lewes, 1997), p. 159.

12 Elizabeth David, *Syllabubs and Fruit Fools* (London, 1969), p. 14.

13 Ivan Day, 'Syllabub Revisited and Sugar Plumb Theories', http://foodhistorjottings.blogspot.co.uk, accessed 26 January 2016. Mr Day has a wealth of information about syllabubs and other historic foods on his blog and website, www.historicfood.com.

14 Hannah Glasse, *The Art of Cookery Made Plain & Easy* [1796] (Hamden, CT, 1971), pp. 327–8.

15 Charlotte Bronte, *Shirley* [1849] (London, 1993), p. 459.

16 Raffald, *The Experienced English Housekeeper*, p. 94.

17 Ibid., p. 95.

18 Holly Arnold Kinney, *Shinin' Times at The Fort* (Morrison, CO, 2010), pp. 234–5.

19 Mark Twain, *Life on the Mississippi* [1883] (New York, 2000), p. 179.

20 Doreen G. Fernandez, 'Carabao Milk in Philippine Life', in *Milk: Beyond the Dairy: Proceedings of the Oxford Symposium on Food and Cookery 1999*, ed. Harlan Walker (Totnes, 2000), p. 120.

21 Hannah Glasse, *The Art of Cookery Made Plain and Easy* [1796] (Wakefield, Yorkshire, 1971), pp. 330–35.

22 Louisa May Alcott, *Little Women* (New York, 1962), p. 62.

23 Maria Parloa, *Miss Parloa's Young Housekeeper* (Boston, MA, 1894), p. 291.

24 Terence Scully, ed., *The Viandier of Taillevent* (Ottawa, 1988), p. 166.

25 Alcott, *Little Women*, p. 62.

26 Henry William Lewer, ed., *A Book of Simples* (London, 1908), p. 128.

27 Martin, *Dairy Queens*, pp. 136–7.

28 Carol Wilson, 'Cheesecake', in *The Oxford Companion to Sugar and Sweets*, ed. Darra Goldstein (New York, 2015), pp. 125–6.

29 Terence Scully, *The Neapolitan Recipe Collection* (Ann Arbor, MI, 2000), pp. 158–9.

30 Irving Cobb, 'Speaking of Operations –', in *This is My Best* (New York, 1942), p. 844.

31 Allison Meier, 'The Frost Fair: When the River Thames Froze Over Into London's Most Debaucherous Party', www.atlasobscura.com, accessed 2 March 2016.

32 Joseph Addison, *The Tatler*, no. 148 (London, 1709), p. 124, available at http://quod.lib.umich.edu, accessed 2 March 2016.

33 Anonymous, *A Propre New Booke of Cookery* (London, 1545), unpaginated.

34 Hannah Woolley, *The Queen-like Closet or Rich Cabinet Stored with All Manner of Rare Receipts for Preserving, Candying and Cookery.*

Very Pleasant and Beneficial to all Ingenious Persons of the Female Sex (London, 1672), recipe number 93.

35 Wayne Heisler, 'Kitsch and the Ballet Schlagobers', *Opera Quarterly*, XXII/1 (Winter 2006), pp. 38–64.

36 Woolley, *The Queen-like Closet*, recipe number 57.

37 John Florio, *A Worlde of Wordes, or, Most Copious, and Exact Dictionarie in English and Italian* (London, 1598), p. 216.

38 Randle Holme, *The Academy of Armory* (Chester, 1688), available at Early English Books Online, http://quod.lib.umich.edu, accessed 2 March 2016.

39 Estelle Woods Wilcox, *Buckeye Cookery: With Hints on Practical Housekeeping* (Minneapolis, MN, 1881), p. 163.

40 Oliver Wendell Holmes, *Elsie Venner: A Romance of Destiny* (Boston, MA, 1891), vol. II, p. 110.

41 Helen Saberi and Alan Davidson, *Trifle* (Totnes, 2001), pp. 95–104.

42 Amelia Simmons, *American Cookery* (Hartford, CT, 1798), p. 33, available at http://digital.lib.msu.edu, accessed 14 March 2016.

43 Ibid., p. 105.

44 Rachel Laudan, 'Tres Leches Cake', in *The Oxford Companion to Sugar and Sweets,* pp. 740–41.

45 John Earle, *Microcosmography; Or, A Piece of the World Discovered; in Essays and Characters* (London, 1811), p. 106, available at www.gutenberg.org, accessed on 2 March 2016.

46 Alan Davidson, *The Oxford Companion to Food* (Oxford, 1999), pp. 237–8.

47 H. Syer Cuming, 'Syllabub and Syllabub-vessels', in *The Journal of the British Archeological Association*, vol. XLVII (London, 1891), pp. 212–15.

48 Cuming was also the person who alleged that Mrs Glasse was a nom de plume for one Sir John Hill, an English writer and botanist. Of course, that was not true. Some men of the era persisted in believing that women were not capable of creating a book like that written by Mrs Glasse, despite the many female writers who had proved them wrong.

FOUR THE PROSE AND POETRY OF DESSERT

1 Isabella Beeton, *The Book of Household Management* (London, 1861), Entry #1509, www.gutenberg.org, accessed 24 April 2016.

2 John Florio, *Queen Anna's New World of Words, or Dictionarie of the Italian and English Tongues* (London, 1611), p. 513.

3 Elizabeth Raffald, *The Experienced English Housekeeper* (Manchester, 1769), p. 228.

4 M. Emy, *L'Art de bien faire les glaces d'office* (Paris, 1768), p. 210.

5 George Sala, *The Thorough Good Cook* (London, 1895), p. 73.

6 Chitrita Banerji, *Eating India: An Odyssey into the Food and Culture of the Land of Spices* (New York, 2007), pp. 138–40.

7 Pellegrino Artusi, *Science in the Kitchen and the Art of Eating Well*, trans. Murtha Baca and Stephen Sartarelli (Toronto, 2004), p. 545.

8 Andrew W. Tuer, *Old London Street Cries* (London, 1885), pp. 59–60.

9 Frederick T. Vine, *Ices: Plain and Decorated* (London, [1900?]), p. 6.

10 Ralph Selitzer, *The Dairy Industry in America* (New York, 1976), p. 99.

11 Jules Gouffé, *The Royal Book of Pastry and Confectionery* (London, 1874), pp. v–vi.

12 Ibid., p. vi.

13 Alexis Soyer, *The Gastronomic Regenerator* (London, 1847), p. 628.

14 Raffald, *The Experienced English Housekeeper*, p. 226.

15 Eliza Acton, *Modern Cookery in all Its Branches* (Philadelphia, PA, 1845), p. 373.

16 Ibid., p. 358. According to Laura Mason, writing in *The Oxford Companion to Food* (London, 1999), p. 654, ratafia was a popular seventeenth- and eighteenth-century cordial or brandy-based liqueur usually flavoured with bitter almonds. It was also the name of biscuits, or cookies, similar to macaroons, which were also flavoured with bitter almonds. They may have been called 'ratafia' because of the flavouring they shared with the drink or because they were also served along with the drink.

17 Henriette Davidis, *German National Cookery for American Kitchens* (Milwaukee, WI, 1904), p. 371.

18 T. Percy Lewis and A. G. Bromley, *The Victorian Book of Cakes* [1904] (New York, 1991), p. 60.

19 Sam Sifton, 'The Melting Point', *New York Time Magazine* (New York, 2016), pp. 28–9.

20 Marion Harland, *Breakfast, Luncheon and Tea* (New York, 1875), p. 327.

21 Mrs A. B. Marshall, *Fancy Ices* (London, 1894), p. 117.

22 Soyer, *The Gastronomic Regenerator*, p. 495.

23 Theodore Francis Garrett, ed., *The Encyclopædia of Practical Cookery: A Complete Dictionary of all Pertaining to the Art of Cookery and Table Service* (London, 1898), p. 157.

24 Ursula Heinzelmann, 'Oetker', in *The Oxford Companion to Sugar and Sweets*, ed. Darra Goldstein (New York, 2015), p. 491.

25 Mrs Stephen Gilman, 'Election Cake (My Great Grandmother's', in Royal Baking Powder, Co., *My Favorite Receipt Co.* (New York, 1895), p. 95.

26 Royal Baking Powder, Co., *My Favorite Receipt*, p. 50.

27 Personal communication, 2016.

28 A. A. Milne, *When We Were Very Young* (New York, 1992), p. 48.

29 Urbain Dubois, *Artistic Cookery: A Practical System for the Use of the Nobility and Gentry and for Public Entertainments* (London, 1887), p. 162.

30 Beeton, *The Book of Household Management*, Entry #1237.

31 Peter Brears, *Jellies and their Moulds* (Totnes, 2010), pp. 121–3.

32 Michael Krondl, 'Baker's', in *The Oxford Companion to Sugar and Sweets*, p. 45.

33 Alexandra Leaf, 'Chocolate, Post-Columbian', in *The Oxford Companion to Sugar and Sweets*, pp. 144–7.

34 Maria Willett Howard, *Lowney's Cook Book* (Boston, MA, 1907), p. 265, available at https://ia601406.us.archive.org, accessed June 22, 2016.

35 Francine Kirsch, 'Over the Top: The Extravagant Confectionery of J. M. Erich Weber', *Gastronomica*, IV (2004).

36 Lewis and Bromley, *The Victorian Book of Cakes*, p. 51.

37 Frederick T. Vine, *Saleable Shop Goods for Counter-tray and Window: (Including 'Popular Penny Cakes'). A Practical Book for All in the Trade* (London, 1907), p. 7.

38 Ibid., p. 11.

39 Maria Parloa, *Miss Parloa's New Cook Book and Marketing Guide* (Boston, MA, 1880), p. iv.

40 Rare Book Division, The New York Public Library, 'DINNER [held by] ASTOR HOUSE [at] "[NEW YORK, NY]" (HOTEL)', *New York Public Library Digital Collections*, 1851–1859, http://digitalcollections.nypl.org, accessed 13 June 2016.

41 Rare Book Division, The New York Public Library, 'DAILY MENU [held by] THE GRANVILLE [at] "ST. LAWRENCE-ON-SEA, THANET, ENGLAND" (HOT;)', *New York Public Library Digital Collections*, 1886, http://digitalcollections.nypl.org/items, accessed 13 June 2016.

42 Rare Book Division, The New York Public Library. 'DINNER [held by] [KING LEOPOLD II OF BELGIUM AND QUEEN MARIE-HENRIETTE] [at] BRUXELLES (FOREIGN;)', *New York Public Library Digital Collections*, 1894, http://digitalcollections.nypl.org/items, accessed 13 June 2016.

FIVE DEVELOPING DESSERTS

1 Gillian Riley, *The Oxford Companion to Italian Food* (New York, 2001), pp. 358–9.

2 William Woys Weaver, 'Gugelhupf', in *The Oxford Companion to Sugar and Sweets*, ed. Darra Goldstein (New York, 2015), pp. 311–12.

3 Michael Krondl, 'Baba au rhum', in *The Oxford Companion to Sugar and Sweets*, p. 41.

4 Michael Krondl, *Sweet Invention: A History of Dessert* (Chicago, IL, 2011), p. 188.

5 Marcel Proust, *Remembrance of Things Past*, trans. C. K. Scott Moncrieff and Terence Kilmartin, (New York, 1981), p. 50.

6 Nicola Humble, *Cake: A Global History* (London, 2010), pp. 42–3.

7 Trine Hahnemann, 'Scandinavia', in *The Oxford Companion to Sugar and Sweets*, pp. 597–9.

8 Joyce Toomre, *Classic Russian Cooking: Elena Molokhovets' A Gift to Young Housewives* (Bloomington, IN, 1992), pp. 406–7.

9 Ursula Heinzelmann, 'Black Forest Cake', in *The Oxford Companion to Sugar and Sweets*, p. 65.

10 Anne Willan, 'France', in *The Oxford Companion to Sugar and Sweets*, pp. 268–74.

11 Greg Patent, 'Chiffon Cake', in *The Oxford Companion to Sugar and Sweets*, p. 131.

12 Barbara Wheaton, 'The Endangered Cuisinière Bourgeoise', in *Disappearing Foods*, ed. Harlan Walker, Oxford Symposium on Food and Cookery 1994 Proceedings (Blackawton, Devon, 1995), pp. 221–6.

13 This is a rich and moist cake. I added a half-teaspoon of almond extract to enhance the flavour and sprinkled a little sanding sugar over the almonds. I baked it in a 20-cm (8-in) springform pan at 175°C (350°F), for an hour and fifteen minutes.

14 Krondl, *Sweet Invention*, pp. 286–94.

15 Celestine Eustis, *Cooking in Old Creole Days* (New York, 1903), p. 82.

16 Carolyn Bánfalvi, *The Oxford Companion to Sugar and Sweets*, pp. 223–4.

17 Greg Patent, 'Angel Food Cake', in *The Oxford Companion to Sugar and Sweets*, p. 14.

18 Personal communication, 2013.

19 Eric Rath, 'Japanese Baked Goods', in *The Oxford Companion to Sugar and Sweets*, pp. 374–5.

20 Nina Simonds, 'Mooncake', in *The Oxford Companion to Sugar and Sweets*, pp. 461–2.

21 William Grimes, 'Baked Alaska', in *The Oxford Companion to Sugar and Sweets*, pp. 44–5.

22 Alan Davidson, *The Oxford Companion to Food* (Oxford, 1999), p. 440.

23 Joseph Wechsberg, *The Cooking of Vienna's Empire* (New York, 1968), p. 197.

24 Michael Krondl, *Sweet Invention*, p. 252.

25 Alexis Soyer, *The Gastronomic Regenerator: A Simplified and Entirely New System of Cookery* (London, 1847), p. 478.

26 Ibid., p. 550.

27 Ibid., p. 558.

28 Robert May, *The Accomplisht Cook or The Art and Mystery of Cookery* (London, 1685), p. 238.

29 Amelia Simmons, *The First American Cookbook* [1796] (New York, 1958), p. 34.

30 Geraldene Holt, 'Icing', in *The Oxford Companion to Sugar and Sweets*, pp. 353–4.

31 Agnes Marshall, *Mrs A. B. Marshall's Cookery Book* (London, 1888), p. 41.

32 Theodore Francis Garrett, *The Encyclopaedia of practical cookery: a complete dictionary of all pertaining to the art of cookery and table service: including original modern reciepts for all kinds of dishes for general, occasional, and exceptional use, the making of every description of table confectionery, the home manufacture of wines, liqueurs, and table waters, the laying, decorating, and preparing of banquets, wedding breakfasts, luncheons, teas, celebration and ball suppers, picnics, garden-party refreshments, race and boating baskets, &c.: the care and good management of the cellar, butler's pantry, larder, ice rooms and chests, &c.* (London, 1898), pp. 136–48.

33 Anastasia Edwards, 'Biscuits, British', in *The Oxford Companion to Sugar and Sweets*, pp. 63–4.

34 Stuart and Jenny Payne, *Nicey and Wifey's Nice Cup of Tea and a Sit Down* (Bath, 2004), p. 67.

35 University of Oxford Text Archive, https://ota.ox.ac.uk, accessed 15 June 2016.

36 Hannah Glasse, *The Art of Cookery Made Plain and Easy* [1796] (Hamden, CT, 1971), pp. 200–260.

37 A Practical Housekeeper and Pupil of Mrs Goodfellow, *Cookery As It Should Be* (Philadelphia, PA, 1856), p. 220.

38 Mrs D. A. Lincoln, *Mrs Lincoln's Boston Cook Book: What To Do and What Not To Do in Cooking* (Boston, MA, 1891), p. 391.

39 Marion Harland, *Breakfast, Luncheon and Tea* (New York, 1875), pp. 205–6.

40 *The New York Times* (3 May 1902), p. 8, http://timesmachine. nytimes.com, accessed 21 June 2016.

41 Darra Goldstein, 'Implements of Eating', in *Feeding Desire: Design and The Tools of the Table, 1500–2005*, ed. Darra Goldstein (New York, 2006), p. 139.

42 William C. Conant, 'The Silver Age', *Scribner's Monthly, An Illustrated Magazine for The People*, IX/2 (December 1874), pp. 193–209, available at http://ebooks.library.cornell.edu, accessed 16 May 2016.

43 Goldstein, 'Implements of Eating', p. 148.

44 Ibid., p. 143.

45 Conant, 'The Silver Age', p. 208.

46 Ibid.

SIX THE CONSTANCY OF CHANGE

1 Darra Goldstein, 'Implements of Eating', in *Feeding Desire: Design and the Tools of the Table, 1500–2005* (New York, 2006), p. 155.

2 Margery Wilson, *Pocket Book of Etiquette* (New York, 1937), cited in Arthur M. Schlesinger, *Learning How to Behave: A Historical Study of American Etiquette Books* (New York, 1946), p. 62.

3 Schlesinger, *Learning How to Behave*, p. 50.

4 A member of the royal staff, *The Private Life of King Edward VII (Prince of Wales, 1841–1901)* (New York, 1901), pp. 257–8, available at https://books.google.com, accessed 5 July 2016.

5 Lady Jekyll, DBE, *Kitchen Essays* (London, 1969), p. 135.

6 Emily Post, *Etiquette: 'The Blue Book of Social Usage'* (New York, 1937), pp. 242–3.

7 Ibid., p. 779.

8 Ibid., pp. 817–23.

9 Ibid., p. 261.

10 Emily Post, *Etiquette in Society, in Business, in Politics and at Home* (New York, 1922), pp. 207–8.

11 Irma S. Rombauer and Marion Rombauer Backer, *Joy of Cooking* (New York, 1975), pp. 760–61.

12 Alice Bradley, *Electric Refrigerator Menus and Recipes* (Cleveland, OH, 1927), p. 40.

13 Elizabeth David, *Syllabubs and Fruit Fools* (London, 1971), p. 11.

14 Alice B. Toklas, *The Alice B. Toklas Cook Book* (New York, 1984), pp. 203–6.

15 Ibid., p. 218.

16 Ibid., p. 3.

17 M.F.K. Fisher, 'How to Cook a Wolf', in *The Art of Eating* (New York, 1990), p. 203.

18 Wendell Sherwood Arbuckle, *Ice Cream* (Westport, CT, 1966), pp. 6–7.

19 Carolyn Wyman, *JELL-O: A Biography* (New York, 2001), pp. 44–5.

20 Laura Shapiro, *Something from the Oven: Reinventing Dinner in 1950s America* (New York, 2004), p. 64.

21 See Your Life 'Confidential Chat', http://archive.boston.com, accessed 6 August 2016.

22 *Better Homes and Gardens Dessert Cook Book* (New York, 1960), p. 144.

23 Ibid., p. 118.

24 Ibid., p. 125.

25 See Immaculate Baking Company website for their mixes, www.immaculatebaking.com, accessed 20 August 2016.

26 Miss Jones Baking Co, www.missjones.co/recipes, accessed 16 August 2016.

27 Simone Beck, Louisette Bertholle and Julia Child, *Mastering the Art of French Cooking* (New York, 1963), pp. vii–viii.

28 Ibid., p. x.

29 Joseph Wechsberg, 'Profiles: La Nature des Choses', *New Yorker* (28 July 1975), p. 34.

30 Anne Willan, 'After Nouvelle: The Changing Look in France', *Monthly Magazine of Food and Wine* (January 1982), p. 16.

31 Raymond Sokolov, 'A Tasteful Revolution', *Natural History* (July 1983), p. 83.

32 *Anthony Bourdain: No Reservations,* Season 4, Episode 17, 'Spain' (18 August 2008).

33 'Carrot, Orange and Mango Spheres with Rose Crystals', www.molecularrecipes.com, accessed 16 August 2016.

34 Mary B. Davis, '"Invisible" Frozen Sweet Goods Sales on Rise in French Catering Sector', *Quick Frozen Foods International* (April 2001).

35 'Boncolac SAS', *European Food Journal*, www.european-food-journal.com, accessed 14 August 2016.

36 Dianne's Fine Desserts, http://diannesfinedesserts.com, accessed 14 August 2016.

37 The Dessert Company, http://thedessertcompany.co.uk, accessed 14 August 2016.

38 Roy Strong, *Feast: A History of Grand Eating* (New York, 2002), p. 197.

39 York Avenue, 'U. P.: An Eight Course Dessert Tasting with Dominique Ansel', http://yorkavenueblog.com, accessed 16 August 2016.

40 'William Curley Master Class: Fôret Noire', www.youtube.com, accessed 13 August 2016.

41 Carlos Barrachina, ed., 'Savoir-faire and Something Else', *So Good . . . The Magazine of Haute Pâtisserie* (July 2016), pp. 150–59.

42 Personal communication via email, 2016.

BIBLIOGRAPHY

Alcott, Louisa May, *Little Women* (New York, 1962)

Anonymous, *A Closet for Ladies and Gentlewomen; or, The Art of Preserving, Conserving, and Candying* (London, 1611)

Anonymous, *The Compleat Cook: Expertly prescribing the most ready ways, whether Italian, Spanish, or French, For dressing of Flesh, and Fish, ordering of Sauces or making of Pastry* (London, 1659)

Anonymous, *Good Huswifes Handmaide, for the Kitchin* (London, 1594)

Anonymous, *The Whole Duty of a Woman; or, an Infallible Guide to the Fair Sex* (London, 1737)

Arbuckle, Wendell Sherwood, *Ice Cream* (Westport, CT, 1966)

Arndt, Alice, ed., *Culinary Biographies* (Houston, TX, 2006)

Artusi, Pellegrino, *Science in the Kitchen and the Art of Eating Well*, trans. Murtha Baca and Stephen Sartarelli (Toronto, 2004)

Atkinson, Kate, *Life After Life* (New York, 2013)

Banerji, Chitrita, *Eating India: An Odyssey into the Food and Culture of the Land of Spices* (New York, 2007)

Beck, Simone, Louisette Bertholle and Julia Child, *Mastering the Art of French Cooking* (New York, 1963)

Beeton, Isabella, *The Book of Household Management* (London, 1861)

Better Homes and Gardens Dessert Cook Book (New York, 1960)

Bradley, Alice, *Electric Refrigerator Menus and Recipes* (Cleveland, OH, 1927)

Brears, Peter, *Food and Cooking in 17th Century Britain: History and Recipes* (Birmingham, 1985)

—, *Jellies and Their Moulds* (Blackawton, Devon, 2010)

Briffault, Eugene, *Paris à table* (Paris, 1846)

Brontë, Charlotte, *Shirley* (London, 1993)

Brown, Peter, and Ivan Day, *Pleasures of the Table: Ritual and Display in the European Dining Room, 1600–1900* (York, 1997)

Bunyard, Edward A., *The Anatomy of Dessert: With a Few Notes on Wine* (New York, 2006)

Carter, Charles, *The Compleat City and Country Cook: or Accomplish'd Housewife* (London, 1732)

Chambers, Ephraim, *Cyclopaedia: Or an Universal Dictionary of Arts and Sciences* (London, 1741)

Clarkson, Janet, *Pie: A Global History* (London, 2009)

Cobb, Irving, *This is My Best* (New York, 1942)

Coffin, Sarah D., ed., *Feeding Desire: Design and the Tools of the Table, 1500–2005* (New York, 2006)

Colquhoun, Kate, *Taste: The Story of Britain Through Its Cooking* (New York, 2007)

Crossley-Holland, Nicole, *Living and Dining in Medieval Paris* (Cardiff, 1996)

Cuming, H. Syer, 'Syllabub and Syllabub-vessels', in *Journal of the British Archeological Association*, XLVII (London, 1891)

Davidis, Henriette, *German National Cookery for American Kitchens* (Milwaukee, WI, 1904)

Davidson, Alan, *The Oxford Companion to Food* (Oxford, 1999)

Davidson, Alan and Jane, trans., *Dumas on Food: Recipes and Anecdotes from the Classic Grand Dictionnaire de Cuisine* (Oxford, 1987)

Dawson, Thomas, *The Good Huswifes Jewell* (London, 1587)

Dickens, Charles, *Pictures from Italy* (Boston, MA, 1868)

Digby, Sir Kenelme, *The Closet of the Eminently Learned Sir Kenelme Digby Kt. Opened* (London, 1671)

Dubois, Urbain, *Artistic Cookery: A Practical System for the Use of the Nobility and Gentry and for Public Entertainments* (London, 1887)

Eales, Mary, *Mrs Mary Eales's Receipts* (London, 1985)

Earle, John, *Microcosmography; or, A Piece of the World Discovered; in Essays and Characters* (London, 1811)

Emy, M., *L'Art de bien faire les glaces d'office* (Paris, 1768)

Eustis, Celestine, *Cooking in Old Creole Days* (New York, 1903)

Field, Elizabeth, *Marmalade: Sweet and Savory Spreads for a Sophisticated Taste* (Philadelphia, PA, 2012)

Fisher, M.F.K., *The Art of Eating* (New York, 1990)

Flandrin, Jean-Louis, *Arranging the Meal: A History of Table Service in France* (Berkeley, CA, 2007)

Florio, John, *A Worlde of Wordes; or, Most Copious, and Exact Dictionarie in English and Italian* (London, 1598)

—, *Queen Anna's New World of Words; or, Dictionarie of the Italian and English Tongues* (London, 1611)

Garrett, Theodore Francis, ed., *The Encyclopædia of Practical Cookery: A Complete Dictionary of all Pertaining to the Art of Cookery and Table Service* (London, 1898)

Glasse, Hannah, *The Art of Cookery Made Plain and Easy* (Hamden, CT, 1971)

Goethe, Johann Wolfgang von, *Italian Journey*, trans. Robert R. Heitner (New York, 1989)

Goldstein, Darra, *Fire and Ice* (New York, 2015)

—, ed., *The Oxford Companion to Sugar and Sweets* (New York, 2015)

Gouffé, Jules, *The Royal Book of Pastry and Confectionery* (London, 1874)

Hall, T., *The Queen's Royal Cookery* (London, 1713)

Harland, Marion, *Breakfast, Luncheon and Tea* (New York, 1875)

Heinzelmann, Ursula, *Beyond Bratwurst: A History of Food in Germany* (London, 2014)

Hess, Karen, *Martha Washington's Booke of Cookery* (New York, 1981)

Heywood, Thomas, *The Fair Maid of the West* (London, 1631)

Hieatt, Constance B. and Sharon Butler, eds, *Curye on Inglysch: English Culinary Manuscripts of the Fourteenth Century (Including The Forme of Cury)* (London, 1985)

Holme, Randle, *The Academy of Armory* (Chester, England, 1688) at Early English Books Online, http://quod.lib.umich.edu

Holmes, Oliver Wendell, *Elsie Venner: A Romance of Destiny* (Boston, MA, 1891)

Howard, Maria Willett, *Lowney's Cook Book* (Boston, MA, 1907)

Humble, Nicola, *Cake: A Global History* (London, 2010)

Işin, Mary, *Sherbet and Spice: The Complete Story of Turkish Sweets and Desserts* (London, 2013)

Jekyll, Lady Agnes, *Kitchen Essays* (London, 1969)

Johnston, Mireille, *The Cuisine of the Sun* (New York, 1979)

Kelly, Ian, *Cooking for Kings: The Life of the First Celebrity Chef* (New York, 2003)

Keoleian, Ardashes H., *The Oriental Cook Book: Wholesome, Dainty and Economical Dishes of the Orient, especially adapted to American Tastes and Methods of Preparation* (New York, 1913)

Kinney, Holly Arnold, *Shinin' Times at the Fort* (Morrison, CO, 2010)

Krondl, Michael, *Sweet Invention: A History of Dessert* (Chicago, IL, 2011)

Latini, Antoni, *Lo scalco alla moderna* (Milan, 1993)

Laudan, Rachel, *Cuisine and Empire: Cooking in World History* (Berkeley, CA, 2013)

Levene, Alysa, *Cake: A Slice of History* (New York, 2016)

Lewis, T. Percy, and A. G. Bromley, *The Victorian Book of Cakes* (New York, 1991)

Lincoln, Mrs D. A., *Mrs Lincoln's Boston Cook Book: What To Do and What Not To Do in Cooking* (Boston, MA, 1891)

Markham, Gervase, *The English Housewife* (London, 1631)

Marshall, Agnes, *Mrs A. B. Marshall's Cookery Book* (London, 1888)

Martin, Meredith, *Dairy Queens: The Politics of Pastoral Architecture from Catherine de Medici to Marie-Antoinette* (Cambridge, MA, 2011)

Massialot, François, *The Court and Country Cook* (London, 1702)

May, Robert, *The Accomplisht Cook; or, the Art and Mystery of Cookery* (London, 1685)

A Member of the Royal Household, *The Private Life of King Edward VII (Prince of Wales, 1841–1901)* (New York, 1901)

Montanari, Massimo, *Cheese, Pears, and History in a Proverb* (New York, 2008)

Moss, Sarah, and Alexander Badenoch, *Chocolate: A Global History*
     (London, 2009)
Nasrallah, Nawal, *Delights from the Garden of Eden: A Cookbook and
     a History of the Iraqi Cuisine* (Bloomington, IN, 2004)
Parloa, Maria, *Miss Parloa's New Cook Book and Marketing Guide*
     (Boston, MA, 1880)
—, *Miss Parloa's Young Housekeeper* (Boston, MA, 1894)
Payne, Stuart and Jenny, *Nicey and Wifey's Nice Cup of Tea and a Sit Down*
     (Bath, 2004)
Post, Emily, *Etiquette: 'The Blue Book of Social Usage'* (New York, 1937)
—, *Etiquette in Society, in Business, in Politics, and at Home* (New York,
     1922)
Power, Eileen, *The Goodman of Paris* (New York, 1928)
Proust, Marcel, *Remembrance of Things Past*, trans. C. K. Scott Moncrieff
     and Terence Kilmartin (New York, 1981)
Rabisha, William, *The Whole Body of Cookery Dissected, Taught, and
     fully manifested Methodically, Artificially, and according to the best
     Tradition of the English, French, Italian, Dutch, &c.* (London, 1673)
Raffald, Elizabeth, *The Experienced English Housekeeper* (Lewes, 1997)
Ramsay, Mrs W. M., *Every-day Life in Turkey* (London, 1897)
Reed, Marcia, ed., *The Edible Monument: The Art of Food for Festivals*
     (Los Angeles, CA, 2015)
Richardson, Tim, *Sweets: A History of Candy* (New York and London,
     2002)
Riley, Gillian, *The Oxford Companion to Italian Food* (New York, 2001)
Robertson, Helen, Sarah MacLeod and Frances Preston, *What Do We
     Eat Now: A Guide to Wartime Housekeeping* (New York, 1942)
Roca, Jordi, *The Desserts of Jordi Roca* (New York, 2015)
Rombauer, Irma S., and Marion Rombauer Backer, *Joy of Cooking*
     (New York, 1975)
Routhier, Nicole, *Foods of Vietnam* (New York, 1989)
Royal Baking Powder Co., *My Favorite Receipt* (New York, 1895)
Saberi, Helen, and Alan Davidson, *Trifle* (Blackawton, Devon, 2001)
Sala, George, *The Thorough Good Cook* (London, 1895)
Schlesinger, Arthur M., *Learning How to Behave: A Historical Study
     of American Etiquette Books* (New York, 1946)
Scott, Sir Walter, *The Journal of Sir Walter Scott* (New York, 1891)
Scully, Terence, ed. and trans., *Chiquart's 'On Cookery': A Fifteenth-century
     Savoyard Culinary Treatise* (New York, 1986)
—, *The Neapolitan Recipe Collection* (Ann Arbor, MI, 2000)
—, *The Viandier of Taillevent* (Ottawa, 1988)
Selitzer, Ralph, *The Dairy Industry in America* (New York, 1976)
Shapiro, Laura, *Something from the Oven: Reinventing Dinner in 1950s
     America* (New York, 2004)
Simmons, Amelia, *American Cookery* (Hartford, CT, 1798)
—, *The First American Cookbook* (New York, 1958)

Solomon, Charmaine, *The Complete Asian Cookbook* (South Yarra,
    Australia, 1982)
Soyer, Alexis, *The Gastronomic Regenerator: A Simplified and Entirely New
    System of Cookery, With Nearly Two Thousand Practical Receipts
    Suited to the Income of All Classes* (London, 1847)
—, *The Modern Housewife or Ménagère* (London, 1851)
Spencer, Colin, *British Food: An Extraordinary Thousand Years of History*
    (London, 2001)
Stefani, Bartolomeo, *L'arte di ben cucinare, et instruire* (Mantua, 1662)
Strong, Roy, *Feast: A History of Grand Eating* (New York, 2002)
Toklas, Alice B., *The Alice B. Toklas Cook Book* (New York, 1984)
Toomre, Joyce, *Classic Russian Cooking: Elena Molokhovets' A Gift to Young
    Housewives* (Bloomington, IN, 1992)
Tuer, Andrew W., *Old London Street Cries* (London, 1885)
Twain, Mark, *Life on the Mississippi* (New York, 2000)
Vehling, Joseph Dommers, *Apicius: Cookery and Dining in Imperial Rome*
    (New York, 1977)
Vine, Frederick T., *Ices: Plain and Decorated* (London, [1900?])
—, *Saleable Shop Goods for Counter-tray and Window: (Including 'Popular
    Penny Cakes'). A Practical Book for All in the Trade* (London, 1907)
Walker, Harlan, ed., *Disappearing Foods: Proceedings of the 1994 Oxford
    Symposium on Food and Cookery* (Blackawton, Devon, 1995)
—, *Milk: Beyond the Dairy: Proceedings of the 1999 Oxford Symposium on
    Food and Cookery* (Devon, 2000)
Wechsberg, Joseph, *The Cooking of Vienna's Empire* (New York, 1968)
Wheaton, Barbara Ketcham, *Savouring the Past: The French Kitchen and
    Table from 1300 to 1789* (London, 1983)
Wilcox, Estelle Woods, *Buckeye Cookery: With Hints on Practical
    Housekeeping* (Minneapolis, MN, 1881)
Willan, Ann, with Mark Cherniavsky and Kyri Claflin, *The Cookbook
    Library* (Berkeley, CA, 2012)
Wilson, C. Anne, ed., *Banquetting Stuffe: The Fare and Social Background
    of the Tudor and Stuart Banquet* (Edinburgh, 1991)
Woloson, Wendy, *Refined Tastes: Sugar, Confectionery, and Consumers
    in Nineteenth-century America* (Baltimore, MD, 2002)
Woolley, Hannah, *The Queene-like Closet or Rich Cabinet: Stored with All
    Manner of Rare Receipts for Preserving, Candying and Cookery. Very
    Pleasant and Beneficial to all Ingenious Persons of the Female Sex*
    (London, 1684)
Wyman, Carolyn, *JELL-O: A Biography* (New York, 2001)
Young, Arthur, *Travels during the Years 1787, 1788, and 1789, Undertaken more
    particularly with a View of ascertaining the Cultivation, Wealth, Resources,
    and National Prosperity of the Kingdom of France* (Dublin, 1793)
Young, Carolin C., *Apples of Gold in Settings of Silver: Stories of Dinner as
    a Work of Art* (New York, 2002)
Younger, William, *Gods, Men, and Wine* (Cleveland, OH, 1966)

PERIODICALS

Addison, Joseph, *The Tatler*, 148 (1709)

Barrachina, Carlos, ed., 'Savoir-faire and Something Else', *So Good . . . The Magazine of Haute Pâtisserie* (July 2016)

Conant, William C., 'The Silver Age', *Scribner's Monthly, An Illustrated Magazine for The People*, IX/2 (December 1874)

Davis, Mary B., '"Invisible" Frozen Sweet Goods Sales on Rise in French Catering Sector', *Quick Frozen Foods International* (April 2001)

Eigeland, Tor, 'Arabs, Almonds, Sugar and Toledo"', *Saudi Aramco World* (May/June 1996)

Kirsch, Francine, 'Over the Top: The Extravagant Confectionery of J. M. Erich Weber', in *Gastronomica: The Journal of Food and Culture* (2004)

Sifton, Sam, 'The Melting Point', *New York Times Magazine* (2016)

Sokolov, Raymond, 'A Tasteful Revolution', *Natural History* (July 1983)

Wechsberg, Joseph, 'Profiles: La Nature des Choses', *The New Yorker* (28 July 1975)

Willan, Anne, 'After Nouvelle: The Changing Look in France', *Monthly Magazine of Food and Wine* (January 1982)

Whitaker, Ashlee, 'Dairy Culture: Industry, Nature and Liminality in the Eighteenth-century English Ornamental Dairy', *All Theses and Dissertations*, Paper 1327 (2008), available at http://scholarsarchive. byu.edu.

PAMPHLETS

Auto Vacuum Frozen Dainties (New York, *c.* 1910)

David, Elizabeth, *Syllabubs and Fruit Fools* (London, 1971)

WEBSITES

Boston.com 'Your Life'
http://archive.boston.com

The Dessert Company
http://thedessertcompany.co.uk

Dianne's Fine Desserts
http://diannesfinedesserts.com

European Food Journal
www.european-food-journal.com

Feeding America
http://digital.lib.msu.edu/projects/cookbooks/index.cfm

Immaculate, Honestly Delicious
www.immaculatebaking.com

Ivan Day, 'Syllabub Revisited and Sugar Plumb Theories'
http://foodhistorjottings.blogspot.co.uk

Miss Jones Baking Co.
www.missjones.co/recipes

Molecularrecipes.com
www.molecularrecipes.com

The National Trust
www.nationaltrust.org.uk

New York Times archive
https://timesmachine.nytimes.com/browser

Rare Book Division, The New York Public Library
http://digitalcollections.nypl.org

University of Oxford Text Archive
http://ota.ox.ac.uk

'William Curley Master Class – Fôret Noire – You Tube'
www.youtube.com

York Avenue, U. P.: An Eight Course Dessert Tasting with Dominique Ansel
http://yorkavenueblog.com

ACKNOWLEDGEMENTS

People love dessert – making it, eating it and talking about it. When I told friends and acquaintances about this book, I discovered how much people enjoy reminiscing about childhood favourites, describing desserts they love as well as those they merely tolerate (fruitcake and honey cake in particular), and sharing new discoveries. I thank them all for their suggestions, stories and eagerness to taste desserts with me.

I especially want to thank Ken Albala, Madonna Berry, Kyri Claflin and Michael Krondle for their close readings of the manuscript. They not only offered encouragement, which is always welcome, but picked nits, sent me back to sources and made this a better book than it would have been without them. I'm also indebted to Andrew F. Smith for suggesting dessert as a topic and being so supportive over the years.

Many people happily offered their dessert anecdotes and recipes, some of which are included in the book. Thanks especially to Emily Beck, Maylun Buck-Lew, Roz Cummins, Ursula Heinzelmann, Holly Korda, Larry Newhouse, Paula Rosenstock, Yoshio Saito, Albena Shkodrova, Agni Thurner and Vrinda Varma for the deliciousness they shared.

Both friends and individuals I've only met in the ether graciously supplied wonderful images. My thanks to William Curley, Peggy De Muth, Richard Doughty, Lori Gately, Sarah Jones, Judy Kales, Holly Arnold Kinney, Susan McLellan Plaisted and Paul Wood.

As always, I appreciate the ever-patient and constructively critical members of my writing group – Myrna Kaye, Roberta Leviton, Barbara Mende, Shirley Moskow and Rose Yesu. They deserve thanks and ice cream.

I owe many others thanks for their support past, present and (I hope) future. They include Gary Allen, Marylène Altieri, Jackie and Parviz Amirhor, Chitrita Banerji, Marilyn Brass, Sheila Brass, Marianne Brown, Joe Carlin, Anita Denley, Jane Dixon, Anne Faulkner, Kathleen Fitzgerald, Kathleen Flynn, Darra Goldstein, Dawn Hayes, Jeanne and Jim Hupprich, Sarah Hutcheon, Janet Katz, the MacLeod clan – Dan, Doug, Lola, Scott, Rachel, Shannon and Dylan – Deb McDonald, Ellen Messer, Doris Millan, Sabra Morton, Jill Norman, Susan Rossi-Wilcox, Lynn Schweikart, Max Sinsheimer,

Keith Stavely, Nancy Stutzman, Beth Surdut, Elisabeth Townsend, Molly Turner, Bruce Williams, Winnie Williams, Jane and John Wilson, Johnnie Wolfson and the members of the Culinary Historians of Boston.

They should all have a second helping of their favourite dessert.

PHOTO ACKNOWLEDGEMENTS

The author and the publishers wish to express their thanks to the below sources of illustrative material and/or permission to reproduce it.

Evan Amos: p. 38; Author's Collection: pp. 126, 185; Ra Boe: p. 46; Boston Public Library – Digital Commonwealth: pp. 13, 133, 136, 137, 145, 146, 153, 193, 204, 211; © The Trustees of the British Museum, London: pp. 22, 51, 53, 73, 82, 102, 106, 125, 129; Johan Bryggare: p. 161 (top); Popo Le Chien: p. 163; courtesy of William Curley, Patissier-Chocolatier: pp. 6, 31, 218, 228; courtesy of Peggy De Muth: p. 81 (right); photograph by Tor Eigeland for Saudi Aramco World/SAWDIA: pp. 60–61, 62; Getty Images: pp. 43 (DEA/A. Dagli Orti), 84 (SSPL), 207 (Popperfoto); Getty Research Institute: pp. 48, 57, 68, 69, 72, 75; Ginnerobot: p. 214; Thomas Högner Maximilian Högner: p. 147; iStockphoto: p. 220 (VvoeVale); courtesy of Judy Kales: pp. 81 (left), 221; JW: p. 161 (foot); Katorisi: p. 167; Holly Arnold Kinney: p. 94; Library of Congress, Washington, DC: pp. 28, 127, 139, 192, 206, 230; Lotus Head: p. 203; M: p. 148; Metropolitan Museum of Art, New York: p. 158; courtesy Miss Jones Baking Co.: pp. 212, 215 (Larisas Erin Greer); Katrin Morenz: p. 165; John Morgan: p. 209; Ewan Munro: p. 104; Museum of Fine Arts, Boston: p. 64; New York Public Library: p. 156; © Omni Parker House Parkives: p. 174; Ox010C: p. 162; REX Shutterstock: pp. 111 (Woman's Weekly), 142 (Kharbine-Tapabor), 179 (Food and Drink); Sandstein: p. 237; Shutterstock: pp. 25 (Marcin Jucha), 80 (Esin Deniz), 91 (skoraq), 96 (AGCreations), 116 (Everett), 117 (sarsmis), 168 (AnjelikaGr), 171 (Anita Huszti), 172 (Kaimirov Vladimir), 176 (Margaret Tong), 177 (juefraphoto), 191 (marouillat photo), 200 (Hans Geel), 223 (Kondor83); Silar: p. 184; SKopp: p. 98; Smithsonian Libraries, Washington, DC: p. 77; Spode Museum Trust: p. 115; Tourismus Salzburg: p. 170; © Victoria and Albert Museum, London: pp. 14, 24, 33, 40, 45, 89, 124, 130, 131, 144 (left and right), 160, 187, 197; Wellcome Images: p. 120; Wmienhart: p. 217.

INDEX

Page numbers in *italics* refer to illustrations